Walt and Frances, Thanksgiving, 2012, their last photo together.

For a long time I have wanted to publish a cookbook for my family and friends and now with the help of my dear friend, Mike Simpson, I am getting to fulfill my dream.

In this book you will find treasured family recipes, many that have been shared by friends and some that I have just collected along the way. When you use this book, as I hope you will, remember those who have helped to make it possible.

Through the years I have enjoyed having you as my family and friends and I want you to know that I love you and treasure you more then you will ever know.

Good Cooking!

Table of Contents

Appetizers

Breads

Cakes

Candy and Nuts

Cookies

Desserts

Dressings

Drinks

Egg Dishes

Meats

Pickles and Relishes

Pies

Salads

Soups

Vegetables

Appetizers

Alice Storey's Cheese-Olive Balls

½ lb grated sharp cheddar cheese
4 T butter
1 c flour
Dash cayenne pepper
Dash salt
1 6oz jar pimento-stuffed olives

Cream cheese and butter. Add flour and spices. Pack pastry around each olive. Bake 350° 15 min or until lightly brown.
Serve warm

Freeze before baking if you wish.

Aunt Maude Holt's Nut Balls

1 c flour
1 c nuts (ground)
2 T white sugar
1 stick butter
1 t vanilla
Pinch of salt

Cream butter, sugar, flour and then add nuts, salt and vanilla. Shape in balls about the size of a marble. Bake at 325° about 15-20 min. May be dusted with powdered sugar.

Bacon Cheddar Puffs

1 c milk
¼ c butter
1 c flour
4 large eggs
1 c shredded sharp cheddar cheese

8 slices bacon, cooked, crumbled
½ t onion salt or powder
¼ t garlic salt
¼ t black pepper

Combine milk and butter in medium saucepan. Cook over medium heat, stirring often until butter is melted and mixture is simmering. Add flour, stir until mixture forms a ball. Remove from heat. Beat in 1 egg at a time until mixture is smooth. Stir in remaining ingredients; mix well. Drop heaping teaspoons of mixture onto greased baking sheet. Bake in preheated 350°F oven 25 min or until puffed and golden brown. Serve warm or at room temperature.
Makes 3 doz. appetizers.

Dinner at the Krites' Home on Green Street

Barbecue Chicken Bites

1 egg
2 T milk
4 c crushed barbecue potato chips
½ lb boneless skinless chicken breasts
    cut into 1½ in cubes
Barbecue sauce

In a shallow bowl, whisk egg and milk. Place potato chips in another bowl. Dip chicken in egg mixture, then roll in chips. Place in single layer on a greased baking sheet. Bake at 400° for 10-15 min or until juices run clear. Serve with barbecue sauce.
    Yield: 4 servings

Bite-Size Cheese Balls

1 3 oz cream cheese, softened
1 c shredded cheddar cheese
¾ c shredded carrot
1 t honey
½ c finely chopped pecan
24 pretzel sticks

Combine first 4 ingredients; cover and chill 1 hour. Shape into 1 in balls and roll in pecans. Cover and chill. To serve, place a pretzel into each.
    Yield: 2 doz.

Murphy Family

BLT Bites

16-20 cherry tomatoes
1 lb. bacon, cooked and crumbled
½ c mayonnaise
⅓ c chopped green onions
3 t grated Parmesan cheese
2 T snipped fresh parsley

Cut a thin slice off of each tomato top. Scoop out and discard pulp. Invert tomatoes on a paper towel to drain. In a small bowl, combine the remaining ingredients; mix well. Spoon into tomatoes. Refrigerate for several hours.
Yield 16 - 20 appetizer servings

Cheddar Ham Cups

2 c (8oz) finely shredded cheddar cheese
5 oz thinly sliced deli ham, chopped
3/4 c mayonnaise
1/3 c real bacon bits
2 - 3 t Dijon mustard
1 tube (12oz) large flaky biscuits

In a bowl, combine the cheese, ham, mayonnaise, bacon and mustard. Split biscuits into thirds. Press onto the bottom and up the sides of ungreased miniature muffin cups. Fill each with about 1 T of cheese mixture.

Bake at 450° for 9-11 min. or until golden brown and the cheese is melted. Let stand 2 min. before removing from the pans. Serve warm.

Yield 2½ doz.

Frances Krites

Cheese and Olive Spread

Mix 1 8oz shredded mild Cheddar Cheese
1 8oz cream cheese, softened,
½ c mayonnaise
¼ c Each chopped stuffed green olives
and green onions
2 T lemon juice and
¼ t ground red pepper.

Refrigerate. Serve with crackers

June Lyon's Dip

Kraft cheese grated (about ½ lb)
1 can Rotel chili and tomatoes

Heat together until cheese
melts and mixture is
spreadable.
Serve with Scoops.

Cheese Ball

1 8oz cream cheese, softened
1 8oz spreadable chive and
olive cream cheese
2 c (8oz) sharp shredded
cheddar cheese
2 t paprika
½ t cayenne pepper

In a small mixing bowl,
beat cream cheese until smooth.
Stir in cheddar cheese, paprika,
and cayenne. Shape into ball;
wrap in plastic wrap.
Refrigerate 4 hours or until
firm.
Serve with apples and crackers
Yield: 2½ cups

Cheese Biscuits

8 oz grated sharp cheddar cheese
2 sticks margarine
¼ t salt
Red pepper or cayenne to taste
2 cups flour
2½ c crushed Rice Krispies

Mix all ingredients together well. Shape into small balls. Place on baking sheet and press flat with fork. Bake on ungreased sheet in 350° oven 10 - 12 min or until light golden brown.

I usually flatten them in my hands before I put them on the sheet.
These are very good -

One of my favorite recipes!

Cheese Crunchies

½ c butter or margarine
3 c shredded cheddar cheese (12 oz)
3 c rice cereal, divided
1 c flour
1 t chili powder
½ t onion powder
¼ t salt

Heat oven to 350°. In a large bowl, cream butter and cheese. Add 2 c cereal, flour and seasonings. Mix well. Divide dough in half. Shape into 2 logs; roll logs in remaining cereal. Chill 30 min. Slice log into ½ in slices; place onto ungreased cookie sheets. Bake 12-14 min or until golden brown.
Yield: 48

(I would crush the cereal a little)

Walter B. Murphy

Cheese Puffs

1 c water
2 T butter
½ t salt
⅛ t cayenne pepper
1 c flour
4 eggs
1¼ c shredded Swiss or Gruyere cheese
1 T Dijon mustard
¼ c grated Parmesan cheese

In large sauce pan, bring water, butter, salt and pepper to a boil. Add flour all at once and stir until a smooth ball forms. Remove from heat and transfer to mixing bowl. Add eggs, one at a time, beating after each addition. Continue beating until mixture is smooth and shiny. Stir in Swiss and mustard.

Drop by rounded teaspoonfuls 2 in. apart onto greased baking sheets. Sprinkle with Parmesan cheese. Bake 425° for 15-20 min. or until golden brown. Serve warm or cold. Yield: 4 doz.

Hot Cheese Tidbits

8 oz cream cheese
½ c butter
1 c flour
⅛ t salt
Dash cayenne pepper
Cheddar cheese cut in small
    pieces about ½ x ½

Cream butter and cream cheese. Add flour, salt and cayenne pepper. Chill. Roll thin. Cut in 2 in squares. Put a piece of cheese in each square. Fold into a triangle. Press edges with a fork. Freeze. Baking time frozen — 450° for 5-7 min.

Yield: 4½ doz.

Cheese Wafers #1

2 c butter or margarine, softened
1 lb shredded Cheddar cheese
4 c flour
½ t salt
1 - 2 t ground red pepper
½ t paprika

Beat butter and shredded Cheddar cheese at med. speed with electric mixer until blended; add flour and remaining ingredients, beating until blended. Cover dough and chill 2 hours.

Shape dough into 4 (8in) logs. cover and chill 8 hours. Cut into ¼ in slices and place on ungreased baking sheets.

Bake at 350° for 15 min. Remove to wire racks to cool. Store in airtight container.

Yield: 10 doz.

Cheese Wafers #2

1 8 oz can Parmesan cheese
2 sticks butter, softened
½ t salt
⅛ t red pepper
2 c flour

Mix well the cheese, butter and salt. Add red pepper and mix well. Stir in flour gradually. The dough will be crumbly - Shape into ¾ in balls. Place 1 in apart on baking sheet. Press each with fork. Bake 325° 10-15 min. Cool.

Yield: 5-6 doz

Cheese Wafers # 3

1 c flour
½ t salt
¾ c chopped pecans or walnuts
2 c (8oz) shredded Cheddar cheese
½ c butter or margarine, softened

Combine first 4 ingredients in mixing bowl; add butter and mix well. Divide dough in half. Shape each half into a 10 in roll. Wrap in waxed paper and chill at least 2 hours.

Slice rolls into ½ in. sticks and place on greased cookie sheets. Bake at 350° for 15 min.

Yield: about 6 doz.

Note: Rolls can be prepared ahead of time and frozen. Soften at room temperature for 1½ hours; slice and bake as directed.

Chicken Nut Puffs

1½ c finely chopped cooked chicken
⅓ c toasted chopped almonds
1 c chicken broth
½ c vegetable oil
2 t Worcestershire sauce
1 T dried parsley flakes
1 t seasoned salt
½ – 1 t celery seed
⅛ t cayenne pepper
1 c flour
4 eggs

Combine chicken and almonds; set aside.
In saucepan combine next 7 ingredients.
Bring to boil. Add flour all at once; stir
until smooth ball forms. Remove from
heat; let stand 5 min. Add eggs one at a
time, beating after each. Beat until
smooth. Stir in chicken and almonds.
Drop by heaping t onto greased
baking sheets. Bake at 450° for
12–14 min. or until golden brown.
Serve warm.
        Yield: About 6 doz.

Christmas Party Pinwheels

2   8oz cream cheese, softened
1   .4oz ranch salad dressing mix
½ c   minced sweet red pepper
½ c   minced celery
¼ c   sliced green onions
¼ c   sliced stuffed olives
3 - 4   flour tortillas (10 in)

In mixing bowl, beat cream cheese and dressing mix until smooth. Add red pepper, celery, onions and olives; mix well. Spread about 3/4 c on each tortilla. Roll up tightly; wrap in plastic wrap. Refrigerate for at least 2 hours. Slice into ½ in pieces.
Yield: 15 - 20 servings

Cream Cheese Kicker

½ jar Harry & David Pepper and
        onion relish
8oz cream cheese, softened

Mix relish and cream cheese until smooth.
For a delicious twist, add drained canned pineapple or chopped nuts.
For a decorative finish, form the mixture into balls and roll in crushed nuts.

Noah and Bertha Krites

Cream Cheese and Olives
Pecan Bites

Stir together 3 oz. softened cream cheese, 1/2 c finely chopped pimiento-stuffed olives, 1 T chopped fresh chives, and 1/4 t. pepper. Spread onto 40 large toasted pecan halves and top with 40 large toasted halves, forming sandwiches.

To toast pecans, preheat oven to 350°. Place pecans in a single layer in a shallow pan until slightly toasted and fragrant, stirring occasionally. This should take about 8-10 min.

Cream Cheese Olive Spread

1 8oz cream cheese, softened
½ c finely chopped pimento-stuffed olives
1 T mayonnaise
½ c chopped pecans
¼ c chopped fresh chives

Stir together cream cheese, olives and mayonnaise. Shape mixture into 2 (6 in) logs; wrap in plastic wrap, and chill at least 30 min. or store in the refrigerator in an airtight container up to 2 days.

Place pecans in single layer in a shallow pan. Bake at 350° for 8 min. or until toasted, stirring occasionally. Let stand 30 to cool.

Roll logs in chopped chives and pecans just before serving.

Creamy Chicken Spread

1 8oz cream cheese, softened
½ c sour cream
1 t dried minced onion
½ t onion salt
½ t Worcestershire sauce
¼ t cayenne pepper
2 10oz cans chunk white chicken, drained

In a mixing bowl, combine the first six ingredients. Fold in chicken. Cover and refrigerate for at least 1 hour. Sprinkle with paprika if desired. Serve with crackers.
Yield: about 3 cups

Fast Goodies

2 c biscuit mix
1 stick butter, melted
1 8oz sour cream
½ c shredded cheddar cheese

Combine all ingredients; mix well. Spoon into tiny greased muffin pans filling ½ full. Bake in 450° oven for 10-12 min or until done.
Makes 4 doz.

Fried Ham Cubes

2 eggs
1 T milk
1½ c dry bread crumbs
½ c grated Parmesan cheese
1 T dried parsley flakes
1½ lb boneless fully cooked ham,
    cut into 1 inch cubes
Oil for frying

In a shallow bowl, beat eggs and milk. In another bowl, combine bread crumbs, Parmesan cheese and parsley. Dip ham cubes in egg mixture, then roll in crumb mixture.

In skillet, heat ¼ of oil to 375°. Fry ham cubes, a few at a time, for 2 min on each side or until golden brown. Drain on paper towels.

Cheese Dipping Sauce

5 oz Velveeta cheese, cubed
¼ c milk
½ c salsa

In small saucepan, heat cheese and milk over med. heat 3-4 min. or until cheese is melted. Remove from heat; stir in salsa. Serve with ham cubes. Can also use ranch dip.

Yield: 3 doz.

Golden Chicken Nuggets

6 whole breasts, skinned and boned
1 c flour
1½ t salt
1 T plus 1 t sesame seeds
2 eggs, slightly beaten
1 c water
Vegetable oil

Cut chicken into 1 X ½ inch pieces; set aside. Combine next five ingredients. Dip chicken into batter and fry in hot oil (375°) until golden brown. Drain on paper towels. Makes 8 – 10 servings.

Ham and Cheese Pinwheels

Cracker Barrel cheddar cheese
Smoked cooked ham (slices)
"Whipped" cream cheese with olives

Cut cheddar cheese into ¼ X ¼ X tin sticks. Spread each ham slice with thin layer of cream cheese. Place cheddar cheese at one edge of ham; roll up. Chill. Cut into ½ inch slices just before serving. Serve on cucumber slices or crackers if desired.

Bertha and Noah Krites with the Murphy Boys

Honey Fruit Dip

1 8 oz cream cheese, softened
1 7 oz jar marshmallow creme
1 T honey
1 t grated orange peel
¼ t ground cinnamon
⅛ t ground nutmeg

In a small mixing bowl combine and beat ingredients until smooth. Serve with fruit. Refrigerate leftovers.
Yield: 2 cups

June Lyon's Appetizers

1 c chopped Vidalia onions
1 c mayonnaise
1 c grated cheddar cheese

Mix. Bake 15 min. at 350°

Serve hot with Scoops.

Spinach Dip

Stir together
8 oz cream cheese
16 oz sour cream
1 can sliced water chestnuts
1 pk. thawed and well drained spinach
1 pk vegetable soup mix

Kathryn Barber's Cheese Dreams

3/4 lt sharp cheddar cheese, grated
2 sticks margarine
3 c flour
1 t salt
Red pepper

Mix cheese and margarine
well. Add other ingredients.
Put through a cookie press
or make into small balls
and flatten. Sprinkle with
paprika before baking in
350° oven about 12 - 15 min.
or until done.

Little Smokie Wraps

2   8oz Crescent rolls
1   16oz Smokies

Separate dough into 8 triangles, cut each lengthwise into 3 triangles Place 1 smokie across the wide end of each triangle; roll toward narrow end to wrap smokie in dough. Place on ungreased baking sheet; dough point down. Bake according to dough package directions. Serve hot or warm.

Biscuits Wraps

These can also be made with refrigerated biscuits. Roll biscuits to thin pastry and cut into strips. Wrap smokies with a piece and place on sheet and bake until golden brown

Louisa Bradshaw's Cheese Cookies

8 oz med. cheddar cheese, grated
½ lb. margarine, softened
3 c flour
1 t dry mustard
¼ t red pepper

Mix cheese and margarine with hands until creamy. Sift dry ingredients; fold in with hands and mix well. Grease cookie sheet lightly. Use a cookie press or roll in small balls and flatten in palms of hands. Bake 350° for 19 - 20 min.
Yield: 4 doz.

Marshmallow Fruit Dip

1 8 oz cream cheese, softened
1 6 oz cherry yogurt
1 8 oz Cool Whip, thawed
1 7 oz jar marshmallow creme

In a small mixing bowl, beat cream cheese and yogurt until blended. Fold in Cool Whip and marshmallow creme. Serve with fruit.
Yield: 5 cups

Fresh Fruit Dip

1 8 oz cream cheese, softened
1 jar marshmallow creme

Mix by hand until smooth.

Mildred Garner's Cheese Crisps
(of the T. W. Garner family that
makes Texas Pete)

1 lb grated sharp cheddar cheese
2 c flour
1¼ c margarine
Dash salt
1 T Texas Pete or to taste
2 c crushed Rice Krispies

Combine all ingredients; blend
well. Roll out between two
pieces of waxed paper. Cut
with small round cutter.
Bake in 350° oven for 17 min
or until done.

Mrs. Marvel Campbell's Cheese Dreams

1 lb sharp cheddar cheese, shredded
2 cups butter
4 cups flour
½ t salt
Hot pepper sauce
Paprika

Cut butter and cheese into
flour (or use food processor).
Add salt and a liberal amount
of hot pepper sauce.
Roll or pat out to about ¼ in
thickness. Cut into tiny shapes
as desired.
Place on ungreased baking
sheet; sprinkle tops with
paprika. Bake in 325° oven
for about 15 min. or until
done. Do not allow to brown.

Olive-Nut Bread Slices

2 1/2 c flour
1 T baking powder
1/2 c sugar
1 c pimiento-stuffed olives, sliced
1 c chopped walnuts
1 2oz jar diced, drained pimiento
1 egg, beaten
1 1/4 c milk
cream cheese

Combine flour, baking powder and sugar; stir well. Add olives, walnuts and pimiento. Stir until well coated. Combine egg and milk and stir into olive mixture. Spoon batter into 6 greased and floured 4 x 2 x 2 in loaf pans. Bake 350° 25-30 min or until golden. Spread slices with cream cheese.

Pecan Cheese Ball

2 8g cream cheese, softened
1 8g crushed pineapple, drained
¼ c chopped green bell pepper
2 t finely chopped onion
2 t seasoned salt
2 c chopped pecans, toasted and divided

Combine first 5 ingredients;
stir in 1 c pecans. Cover and
chill until firm.
Shape mixture into a ball.
Roll in remaining pecans. Place
ball on serving platter.
Serve with crackers and strips
of red and green bell pepper.

Yield 1 (5 in) cheese ball

Pickle and Ham Appetizers

1 12oz cooked ham
1 24oz jar dill spears, drained
1 8oz soft cream cheese

Pat ham and pickle spears
dry with paper towel.
Spread 13 ham slices with
about 1 T cream cheese each.
Top each with 1 pickle spear.
Roll up and refrigerate
1 hour or overnight.
Cut each pickle roll into
4 - 6 pieces to serve.
Makes 62 - 78

Pineapple Cheese Ball #1

2 8oz cream cheese, softened
1 8oz crushed pineapple, drained
¼ c finely chopped green pepper
2 T finely chopped onion
2 t seasoned salt
1½ c finely chopped nuts

In a small mixing bowl, beat cream cheese, pineapple, green pepper, onion and salt until well-blended. Cover and refrigerate overnight. Serve with crackers.
Yield: 1 cheese ball (3 cups)

Pineapple Cheese Ball #2

2 8oz cream cheese
1 8½ oz crushed pineapple, drained
1 t salt
¼ c chopped maraschino cherries
chopped nuts

Mix all ingredients except nuts and form into a ball. Roll in nuts and wrap in Saran Wrap. Put in refrigerator until ready to serve.

Pineapple-Pecan Cheese Spread

2 8 oz cream cheese, softened
1 ½ c (6 oz) shredded cheddar cheese
1 c chopped pecans, toasted, divided
¾ c crushed pineapple, drained
1 can (4 oz) chopped green chilies, drained
2 T chopped roasted sweet red pepper
½ t garlic powder

In a large mixing bowl, beat cream cheese until smooth. Add the cheddar cheese, ¾ c pecans, pineapple, chilies, red pepper and garlic powder; mix well. Transfer to a serving dish. Cover and refrigerate until serving.
Sprinkle with remaining pecans just before serving. Serve with fresh vegetables.
Yield 3¾ cups.

Pineapple Smokies

1 c packed brown sugar
3 T flour
2 t ground mustard
1 c pineapple juice
½ c white vinegar
1 ½ t soy sauce
2 lb miniature smoked sausages

In a large saucepan, combine the sugar, flour and mustard. Gradually stir in the pineapple juice, vinegar and soy sauce. Bring to boil over medium heat; cook and stir for 2 min. or until thickened. Add sausages; stir to coat. Cook, uncovered, for 5 min longer or until heated through. Serve warm.
Yield: About 8 dozen

Krites' Home

Ranch Ham Roll - Ups

2 8oz cream cheese softened
1 envelope ranch salad dressing mix
3 chopped green onions
11 8 in flour tortillas
22 thin slices deli ham

In bowl, beat the cream cheese
and salad dressing mix until
smooth. Add onions; mix well.
Spread about 3 T over each
tortilla; top each with 2 ham
slices. Roll up lightly and
wrap in plastic wrap. Refrigerate
until firm. Unwrap and cut
into ³/₄ in slices.
   Yield: about 7½ doz.

Mrs. Marvel Campbell's Rum or Sherry Balls

1 6 oz bite size Rice Chex, crushed to
    1½ cups
1 cup sifted confectioner's sugar.
1 cup chopped black walnuts
2 T cocoa
⅛ t salt
½ cup white corn syrup
3 T rum or sherry
    Maraschino cherries
    Pitted dates
    Pecan Halves
    Powdered sugar

Combine and blend together thoroughly
the crushed Rice Chex, confectioner's
sugar, walnuts, cocoa, salt, corn
syrup and rum or sherry.
    Wrap small portions of the
mixture around a drained cherry,
date or pecan half. Let
stand awhile and then roll
in powdered sugar.

Sausage Balls

1 lb sausage
¾ - 1 lb grated sharp cheddar cheese
5 c or 20 oz Bisquick
1 c + 2 T buttermilk

Mix thoroughly. Form
into small balls. Bake
on cookie sheet 375° for
20 min or until golden
brown.

Sausage Pinwheels #1

1 lb hot sausage
2 c flour
1 T baking powder
1 t salt
¼ c shortening
⅓ c milk
grated cheese - optional

Combine flour, baking powder and salt. Cut in shortening and add milk. Turn dough onto floured surface. Roll dough into 18 X 12 rectangle. Spread uncooked sausage over dough. Spread grated cheese on top of sausage. Roll dough into jelly-roll fashion starting with the longest side. Cover and refrigerate 1 hour. Slice dough into ¼ inch slices. Bake at 350° 20 min. Makes 3½ dozen.

Sausage Pinwheels #2

1. 8 oz crescent rolls
½ lb uncooked bulk pork sausage
2 T minced chives

Unroll crescent dough on lightly floured surface; press seams and perforations together. Roll into a 14 X 10 in rectangle. Spread sausage to within ½ in. of edges. Sprinkle with chives. Carefully roll up from a long side; cut into 12 slices. Place 1 in apart in an ungreased 15 X 10 X 1 in baking pan. Bake at 375° for 12 - 16 min. or until golden brown.
Yield: 1 doz

Sausage Quiche Squares

1 lb bulk pork sausage
1 c shredded cheddar cheese
1 c shredded Monterey Jack cheese
½ c finely chopped onion
1 4 oz can chopped green chilies
1 T minced jalapeno pepper, optional
10 eggs
1 t chili powder
1 t ground cumin
1 t salt
½ t garlic powder
½ t pepper

In a large skillet, cook sausage until no longer pink. Place in a greased 13 x 9 x 2 in dish. Layer with cheeses, onion, chilies and jalapeno. In a bowl, beat eggs and seasonings. Pour over cheese. Bake, uncovered, at 375° for 18 - 22 min, or until knife comes out clean. Cool 10 min. Cut into 1 in squares.

Yield : about 8 doz.

Use plastic or rubber gloves when cutting hot peppers to protect your hands!

Sweet and Sour Smokies

Slow cooker

2   16oz miniature smoked sausages
2   21oz cherry pie filling
1   20oz pineapple chunks, drained
3 T brown sugar

Place sausages in a slow cooker.
In a bowl combine other ingredients.
Pour over sausages. Cover and
cook on low for 4 hours.
Yield: 16 - 20 servings

Tangy Ham Roll-Ups

1 package Carolina Pride ham
8oz softened cream cheese
1 T fresh or 1 t dried chopped dill
1 jar pimento-stuffed olives

Mix dill with cream cheese.
Spread on ham slices. Place
olives in the center of each ham
slice. Roll and chill for about
an hour. Cut into 1 inch slices.
Serve chilled.

Thresa Brinn's Party Puffs

1 c boiling water
1 stick butter or margarine
1 c self-rising flour
¼ t salt
4 eggs

Melt butter in boiling water.
Add flour and salt at once, stirring
constantly. It will form a big
ball. Remove from heat and
cool slightly. Add eggs one at a
time beating vigorously with
a wooden spoon after each
addition. Drop on a greased
cooking sheet with a teaspoon
(small amount as it rises a lot)
Bake in hot oven 400° for 15 min
Reduce heat to 325° and cook
for 25 min or until golden
brown. Slit on one side
when cool and fill with
chicken salad.

over ⟶

Simple Chicken Salad

Swanson's chunch style mixin chicken
Dice celery
Sweet pickle chips
Mayonnaise

You can add onion and
boiled egg if desired.

Virginia Lee Satterfield's Cheese Jelly Wafers

½ lb cheese (2 c grated and
2 sticks   packed lightly)
          butter or margarine
2½ c flour
dash salt
Jelly

Cream cheese and butter until creamy. Add flour and salt and mix well. Chill for 3 – 4 hours. Roll very thin using flour if necessary. to work with. Cut out with small biscuit or cookie cutter. Put small amount of jelly in center and top with another of the same size. Pinch edges down with a fork as you do pies). Place on lightly greased sheet and bake in 400° about 15 min.

Makes 4 – 5 doz.

Breads

Angel Flake Biscuits

5 c self-rising flour
1 c shortening
¼ c sugar
1 envelope dry yeast
2 T warm water
2 c buttermilk

Stir flour and measure. Blend shortening into flour. Add 2 T warm water into a bowl with yeast and stir slightly. Add yeast mix into flour mix and then the remaining ingredients. Stir slightly until blended. Place dough on lightly floured surface and roll out ½ - ⅔ in. Cut out with 2 in. cutter. Bake in preheated 425° oven until lightly browned. Top with melted butter if desired.

Makes about 40 2 in biscuits

Mrs. Sally Murphy

Banana Nut Bread

½ c margarine, softened
1½ c sugar
2 eggs
1 c mashed ripe bananas (about 2)
2 T milk
1 t vanilla
2 c flour
1 t soda
½ t salt
¾ c chopped pecans

Cream margarine and sugers Add eggs
one at a time. Beat after each. Stir in
bananas, milk and vanilla. Combine
flour, soda and salt. Stir into
banana mixture just until
moistened. Fold in nuts. Pour
into a greased 9 X 5 X 3 in loaf pan.
Bake 325° oven for 65 - 75 min.
or until toothpick comes out clean.
Cool 10 min. in pan. Remove to
wire rack.
    Yield: 1 loaf

Banana Nut Muffins

2 c flour
¼ c sugar
1 T baking powder
½ t salt
1 c milk
1 egg, beaten
⅓ c vegetable oil
¾ c mashed banana
½ c chopped nuts

Preheat oven to 400°. Grease a 12 cup muffin pan. Sift first 4 ingredients into a medium bowl. Mix milk, eggs, oil, bananas and nuts in a small bowl. Pour batter into flour mixture. Mix batter until moistened. Do not overmix. Spoon batter into prepared muffin cups. Bake until golden brown, about 15 min.

Baron Murphy

Biscuits

2 c self-rising flour
¾ c shortening
½ c milk

Place flour in bowl. Add shortening and milk and mix lightly by hand. Roll dough on lightly floured surface. Cut with 1¾ - 2¼ in. round cutter. Place on greased baking sheet. Bake 400° for 18-20 min or until brown on top.

40 biscuits

Blueberry Muffins

1 c flour
3 T sugar
2 t baking powder
½ t salt
1 egg
2 T melted butter
¼ c + 2 T milk
¾ -1 c blueberries

Combine dry ingredients in a bowl. Stir in egg, butter and milk. Quickly fold in blueberries. Spoon batter into buttered muffin cups ¾ full. Bake 20 min in preheated 400° oven. Remove at once.

Makes about 10 large muffins.

Breakfast Buns

2 c flour
3/4 c sugar, divided
1 T baking powder
3 T margarine
2 eggs
1/2 c milk
1 t vanilla
1 c raisins
1/2 t cinnamon

Combine flour, 1/2 c sugar and baking powder; cut in margarine until mixture resembles coarse crumbs. Beat eggs, milk and vanilla; stir into dry ingredients just until moistened. Add raisins. Drop by T onto a greased baking sheet. Combine the cinnamon and remaining sugar; sprinkle over buns. Bake 325° for 20-25 min or until light golden brown. Serve warm.

Yield: 16 servings

Brenda Smith's Savory Squash Muffins

1½ c flour
2 T sugar
1 t baking powder
½ t baking soda
¼ t salt
½ c vegetable oil
2 large eggs
¾ c grated yellow squash
¾ c grated zucchini squash
2 c pepper jack cheese grated

option: Add
1 clove garlic
Dice and add
to batter.

Preheat oven to 350°. Lightly grease muffin cups. In a large bowl, combine first 5 ingredients. Add oil and eggs beating with an electric mixer at medium speed until combined. Add squash. Stir to combine. Add cheese. Stir to combine. Spoon into prepared muffin cups and bake until golden brown.

Makes 12 big muffins. Recipe can be divided.

Buttery Crescents

2 packs active dry yeast
2 c warm milk (110° – 115°)
6½ – 7 c flour
2 eggs, lightly beaten
¼ c margarine, melted and cooled
3 T sugar
1 t salt
Additional melted margarine, optional

In a large bowl, dissolve yeast in milk. Add 4 c flour, eggs, margarine, sugar and salt; beat until smooth. Add enough remaining flour to make a soft dough. Turn out on floured board; knead until smooth and elastic, about 6-8 min. Place in greased bowl and let rise until doubled in size, about 1 hr. Punch dough down and divide in thirds. Roll each into 12 in circle; cut into 12 wedges. Roll up wedges from wide end and place, pointed end down, on greased baking sheets. Cover and let rise until doubled about 30 min. Bake 400° for 12-14 min. or until golden. Brush with margarine if desired.
Yield: 3 doz.

Cheese 'N' Ham Biscuit Drops

4 c (16 oz) shredded cheddar cheese
3 c biscuit mix
1½ c finely chopped cooked ham (10 oz)
½ c Parmesan cheese
2 T minced fresh parsley
⅔ c milk
2 t spicy brown mustard

In large bowl, combine all ingredients; mix well. Shape into 1 inch balls. Place 1 in. apart on greased baking sheets. Bake 350° for 20-25 min or until lightly browned. Serve warm.

Yield: 7 doz

Cheese Biscuits

1 c milk
2 t sugar
⅓ c real mayonnaise
2 c self-rising flour
1 4 oz shredded cheddar cheese

Mix and drop by spoonfuls on greased baking sheet. Spray with Pam and bake at 350° for 30 min. Spray again as soon as they come out of oven.

Cheese Crescents

2 c packaged biscuit mix
1 c shredded sharp cheddar cheese
2 T butter or margarine, melted

Prepare biscuit mix according to package directions. Knead 8-10 times. Roll out on floured surface to 14 in circle. Brush with melted butter; sprinkle with cheese. Cut into 10 pie shaped wedges. Starting at the wide end, roll each wedge to form a cresant. Put crescents, point down, on lightly greased baking sheet. Bake 450° oven about 10 min. or until golden brown. Remove immediately.

Makes 10

Cherry Nut Bread

2 c butter, softened
3 c sugar
5 eggs, separated
1 t vanilla extract
5 c flour
1 t baking soda
½ t baking powder
½ t salt
1 c buttermilk
2 (10 oz) jars maraschino cherries (drained and chopped)
1 c chopped pecans

In a large mixing bowl, cream butter and sugar. Add egg yolks and vanilla; mix well. Combine flour, soda, baking powder and salt. Add to the creamed mixture alternately with buttermilk just until blended (batter will be thick) In small mixing bowl, beat egg whites until stiff peaks form. Fold into batter. Fold in cherries and pecans. Transfer to 4 greased and floured 9 x 4 x 2 in loaf pans. Bake at 350 for 50-55 min. or until toothpick comes out clean and loaves are golden brown. Cool 10 min. before removing from pans to wire racks.   Yield: 4 loaves

Graduation, Salem College, 1943

Chive Biscuits

2 c flour
3 t baking powder
½ t salt
¼ t baking soda
⅓ c butter-flavored shortening
1 c buttermilk
2 T snipped chives

In a small bowl, combine the first 4 ingredients. Cut in the shortening until mixture resembles coarse crumbs. Stir in buttermilk and chives just until moistened. Drop by T 2 in apart on a greased baking sheet. Bake at 450° for 10-12 min. or until lightly brown. Serve warm.

Makes 1 dozen

Chocolate Applesauce Bread

1½ c flour
1¼ c sugar
¼ t baking powder
1 t soda   ¼ t salt
½ t cinnamon
¼ t nutmeg
⅓ c margarine
2 1oz squares unsweetened chocolate
½ c unsweetened apple sauce
2 eggs, beaten
½ c chopped nuts

Combine first 7 ingredients. Mix well and set aside. Melt chocolate and margarine over low heat. Add chocolate mixture, applesauce, eggs and nuts to flour mix and mix well. Pour batter into greased and floured 9x5x3 in loaf pan. Bake 350° 50-55 min or until tester comes out clean. Cool in pan 10 min. Remove and cool on rack.

Makes 1 loaf

Chocolate Banana Loaves

1 box (18.25g) devil's food cake mix
1 c sour cream
½ c water
3 large eggs
1 t cinnamon
1½ c mashed ripe bananas
    (about 4 medium)

Heat oven to 350°. Coat 2 9x5 in loaf pans with non-stick spray. Beat cake mix, sour cream, water, eggs and cinnamon in a large bowl with mixer on low for 30 seconds or until moistened. Scrape down sides of bowl. Beat on medium 2 min. Stir in mashed bananas. Pour into prepared pans. Bake about 40 min. or until cake tests done. Cool in pan 10 min. Remove from pans and turn right side up and cool on rack.

Chocolate Macaroon Muffins

2 c flour
½ c sugar
3 T cocoa
¼ t salt
1 T baking powder
1 egg, beaten
1 c milk
⅓ c vegetable oil
Macaroon filling

Combine first 5 ingredients in a large bowl; make a well in center. Combine egg, milk and oil; add to dry ingredients stirring just until moistened. Spoon into greased muffin pans; filling ⅓ full. Spoon 2 t macaroon filling in center of each muffin cup. Spoon remaining batter over top filling each cup ⅔ full. Bake 400° for 20 min. Serve warm   Yield: 1 doz.

Filling 1 c flaked coconut
       ¼ c sweetened condensed milk
       ¼ t almond extract
Combine all ingredients; mix well. Yield: ½ c

Cinnamon Bread

2 c flour
1 c sugar
2 t baking powder
½ t soda
1½ t cinnamon
1 t salt
1 c buttermilk
¼ c vegetable oil
2 eggs
2 t vanilla

Topping
2 T sugar
1 t cinnamon
2 t margarine

Preheat oven 350°. Grease 9×5×2 in loaf pan. Combine all bread ingredients in a large bowl and beat 3 min. Pour into prepared pan and smooth top.

Combine topping ingredients until crumbly. Sprinkle over batter. Using a knife, cut in light swirling motion to give a marbled effect.

Bake about 50 min. or until toothpick comes out clean. Cool in pan 10 min. and turn out on wire rack.

Cranberry Nut Bread

1 egg, well beaten
1 c milk
2 T butter, melted
3 c sifted flour
½ c sugar
1 t salt
4 t baking powder
1 c cranberries
½ c chopped pecans
1 t vanilla

Mix egg with milk and butter. Sift together flour, ¼ c sugar, salt and baking powder. Add liquid to flour blend. Chop cranberries fine and add remaining ¼ c sugar to them. Fold cranberries, pecans and vanilla into batter. Pour into greased loaf pan. Bake in 350° oven for 1 hour.

Date Bread

1½ c sugar
2¾ c flour
2 t soda
1 t vanilla
½ t salt
1 T melted butter
1½ c boiling water
1 c chopped nuts
2 c chopped dates
1 egg - beaten

Chop dates and pour boiling water over them. After this cools a little, add the soda. Cream the butter and sugar and add the beaten egg. Then add the water from the dates alternately with the flour which has been sifted with the salt. Blend well. Add nuts, dates and vanilla. Bake 350° about 1 hour.

Makes 2 small loaves

Easy and Good Corn Bread

1 c plain corn meal
1 c plain flour
1 c sweet milk
1 T baking powder
3 T mayonnaise
1 t salt

Mix all ingredients gently until moist. Do not beat. Pour immediately into pan that has been lightly coated with oil. Bake at 400° for 30 min.

Easy Cheddar Biscuits

1½ c flour
1 T baking powder
½ t salt
1 T sugar
1 c (4 oz) shredded sharp cheddar cheese
⅓ c shortening
½ c milk

Combine first 4 ingredients until thoroughly mixed. Add cheese and shortening. Gradually add milk and mix mix until dough leaves side of bowl. Turn dough out onto a lightly floured surface. Shape into a ball. Pat or roll to ½ in thick. Cut with 2 in cutter and place on lightly greased baking sheets. Bake biscuits 425° for 10 min or until golden.

Makes 1½ doz.

Easy Cinnamon Biscuits

1 roll refrigerated buttermilk biscuits
1/3 c sugar
1 1/2 t cinnamon
3 T butter

Preheat oven to 425°. Separate biscuits into 10 pieces. Carefully cut each biscuit in half. In a small bowl, mix together sugar and cinnamon. Melt butter in small saucepan and let cool. Dip each biscuit half in melted butter then in sugar - cinnamon mixture. Place biscuit halves on cookie sheet. Bake 10-12 min or until browned.

Makes 20

Easy Yeast Rolls

1 c water
2 c self-rising flour
1 t sugar
1 pk. yeast
1/2 c shortening

Mix ingredients and drop into greased muffin pan. Bake 425° oven until brown.

Helen Webb's Pumpkin Bread

4 eggs, beaten
3 c sugar
1 c oil
1 c pumpkin (2 c)
½ t baking powder
2 t soda
1½ t salt

2 t cinnamon
2 t cloves
2 t nutmeg
3 c flour (sifted)
1 c water
1 c chopped nuts

Beat eggs; add and beat sugar, oil, pumpkin. By hand add dry ingredients alternating with water. Add nuts. Pour into 2 greased and floured loaf pans. Bake 350° for about 1 hour.

Hot Cheesy Biscuits

2 c flour
2 t baking powder
½ t salt
½ t ground red pepper
1 c shredded sharp cheddar cheese
⅓ c shortening
1 c buttermilk (more or less)

Combine first 4 ingredients in a bowl. Cut in shortening until it is pea sized. Add cheese. Stir in buttermilk and mix just until the dry ingredients are moistened. Drop by heaping T onto greased baking sheet. Bake in 450° oven for 8-10 min or until golden brown. Brush tops of biscuits with additional butter if desired.
Makes about 2 dozen

Hush Puppies
Sanitary Fish Market and Restaurant
Morehead City, N.C.

1 lb fine corn meal
1 egg
1 T salt
1 T sugar
Pinch soda
1 c buttermilk

Stir, adding water, to thick
consistency. Drop in deep fat
(preferably peanut oil). Cook
at 375°
Serving for 6 people

Jane Reed's Best Buttermilk Biscuits

2 c flour
1 T baking powder
3/4 t salt
1 t sugar
1/4 t soda
1/3 c Crisco
1 c buttermilk

In a large bowl, sift together first 5
ingredients. Cut shortening into flour mixture
with a pastry blender or fork (can
use your hands) Add buttermilk until
a soft dough forms. Put dough
onto a floured surface and gently
pat to about 3/4 in thick. Cut
with glass or cutter. For crispy
biscuits, place 2 inches apart
on baking sheet. For biscuits
with softer sides, place close
together.
Bake in 475° oven 9 - 12 min.
or until golden brown.

Linda Dawson's Zucchini Corn Bread

1 stick margarine, melted
¼ c oil
½ t sugar
3 eggs beaten
¼ t salt
¾ c cottage cheese
1¼ c self-rising corn meal
¼ c self-rising flour
1 onion chopped
1½ c zucchini, peeled and
                    grated

Combine all ingredients. Bake at 400° for 30 min, or until browned. Use a 10 in. iron skillet.

(You can warm this over)
(and it will stay moist.)

Wedding in Uniform, 1944

Maraschino Cherry Almond Bread

1, 10 oz jar maraschino cherries
½ c butter, softened
¾ c sugar
2 eggs
1 t vanilla extract
2 c flour
1 t baking powder
½ t salt
½ c slivered almonds

Almond Butter
½ c butter, softened
1 T almonds, finely chopped
½ t almond extract

Drain cherries, reserve juice; add water to juice to make ½ c, Cut cherries in quarters blot dry and set aside. In large mixing bowl, cream butter and sugar. Add eggs, one at a time, beating well after each. Beat in vanilla. Combine flour, baking powder and salt; gradually add to creamed mixture alternately with reserved juice, Stir in cherries and almonds, Pour into greased 9 X 5 X 3 in loaf pan. Bake at 350° 50-60 min or till tests done. Cool 10 min. Remove to rack to cool completely. In small bowl, combine almond butter ingredients, Serve with bread. ½ loaf ½ c almond butter

Myrtle Beach, 1949

Maraschino Cherry Nut Bread

¾ c sugar
2 T melted butter
1 egg
1¼ c liquid (from cherries plus milk)
1 c maraschino cherries, drained and chopped
2¼ c sifted flour
3 t baking powder
½ t salt
¼ – ½ c chopped pecans

    Combine all ingredients, mixing lightly. Turn batter into a greased and floured 9x5x2 in loaf pan. Let stand at room temperature for 20 min. Bake in 350° oven for 1 hour or until bread tests done.
    Makes 1 loaf

Mardi Gras Bread

- 1¼ c cooking oil
- 2 c sugar
- 2 eggs
- 2 c shredded carrots
- 1 8 oz crushed pineapple, drained
- 3 c flour
- 1 t baking soda
- 3 t cinnamon
- 1 t salt
- 1 t vanilla extract
- 1 c chopped nuts

Heat oven to 350°. Grease and flour two loaf pans - Beat oil, sugar and eggs well. Add carrots and pineapple. Mix well. Sift dry ingredients and add to wet ingredients. Add vanilla and nuts. Divide batter into the two pans and bake 1 hr. or until a toothpick comes out clean.

Best served with honey butter. 1 stick of really soft butter mixed thoroughly with ¼ c honey.

Makes 2 loaves

Mom Kritex Banana Tea Loaf

2 eggs
3 c crisco
2 med. size ripe bananas
2/3 c sugar
1 3/4 c sifted flour
3/4 t soda
1 1/4 t cream of tartar
1/2 t salt

Put eggs, crisco, bananas and sugar into blender or food processor. Run until contents are smoothly blended – about 30 seconds. Pour mixture over sifted dry ingredients. Mix gently until barely combined. Pour into greased loaf pan. Bake 350° oven about 45 min or until it tests done.

Moravian Snowballs

1 c sugar
3 c milk
1 pound flour
2 t baking powder
1/2 t salt
1/2 t cinnamon and nutmeg each

Mix all ingredients. Drop spoonfuls of batter into deep fat. They will become round balls. Remove from pan when golden brown. Cool and sprinkle with powdered sugar.

Mrs. McIver's Banana Bread

3 mashed bananas
2 eggs
1 c sugar
1 t salt
1 t soda
1½ c flour
1 stick margarine

Beat eggs. Add sugar and bananas. Add melted margarine Add flour, sifted with soda and salt. Pour into greased loaf pan
Let stand for 20 min.
Bake 325° oven for 50 min. to 1 hour.

Peach Muffins

2 c flour
⅔ c brown sugar
3 t baking powder
¼ t soda
¼ t nutmeg
⅓ c melted butter
1 egg
1 c sour cream
⅔ c chopped peaches

Combine dry ingredients. Stir butter, egg and sour cream into dry ingredients. Just to moisten. Fold in peaches. Bake 400° for 15 - 20 min.

Makes 10 - 12 muffins

Pecan Pie Muffins

1 c chopped pecans
1 c packed brown sugar
½ c flour
2 eggs
½ c butter, melted
½ t vanilla flavoring

Combine pecans, sugar and flour in a bowl. In another bowl, beat eggs until foamy; add butter and vanilla Mix well. Stir into dry ingredients, mixing just until moistened. Place baking cups in muffin pans. Fill ⅔ full. Preheat oven 350° and bake muffins for 20-24 min. Remove from pan and place on a rack to cool.
Makes 10 muffins

Pecan Pie Mini Muffins

1 c packed brown sugar
½ c flour
1 c chopped pecans
⅓ c melted butter
2 beaten eggs

In a bowl, combine the sugar, flour and pecans. Set aside. Combine butter and beaten eggs. Stir into brown sugar mixture. Fill greased and floured mini muffin cups ⅔ full. Bake 350° oven for 20-25 min. or until toothpick comes out clean. Immediately remove muffins from pans to wire racks to cool.

Yield: 2½ doz.

Perfectly Easy Dinner Rolls

1 c warm water (105° - 115°)
2 pks. active dry yeast
1 stick butter, melted
½ c sugar
3 eggs
1 t salt
4 - 4 ½ c flour
additional melted butter (optional)

Combine warm water and yeast in a large bowl. Let stand until yeast is foamy, about 5 min. Stir in butter, sugar, eggs and salt. Beat in flour, one cup at a time, until dough is too stiff to mix. May not need all flour. Cover and refrigerate 2 hrs. to 4 days. Grease 9 x 13" in pan. Turn dough out onto a lightly floured board. Divide into 24 equal-size pieces. Roll each into a smooth ball; place in even rows in pan. Cover and let rise double, about 1 hr. Preheat oven to 375°. Bake until golden brown, 15 - 20 min. Brush with melted butter if desired. Break rolls apart to serve.
　　　Makes 2 doz.

Pineapple Banana Bread

- 3 c flour
- 2 c sugar
- 1 t salt
- 1 t baking soda
- 1 t cinnamon
- 3 eggs
- 1¼ c vegetable oil
- 2 t vanilla extract
- 1 can (8 oz) crushed pineapple, drained
- 2 cups mashed bananas (4-5 medium)

In a large bowl, combine the first 5 ingredients. In another bowl, beat the eggs, oil and vanilla; add pineapple and bananas. Stir into the dry ingredients just until moistened. Pour into 2 greased 8 X 4 X 2 in loaf pans.

Bake at 350° for 60-65 min. or until a toothpick comes out clean. Cool for 10 min, before removing from pans to wire rack.

Yield: 2 loaves

Pineapple Biscuits

½ c packed brown sugar
¼ c margarine, softened
1 8oz crushed pineapple, drained
1 t cinnamon
1 12oz refrigerated biscuits

In a bowl combine brown sugar and margarine; stir in pineapple and cinnamon. Spoon into 10 greased muffin cups. Place one biscuit in each prepared cup. Bake at 425° for 10 min. or until golden brown. Let stand 5 min. before inverting onto a serving platter.
Yield: 10 servings

Pineapple – Nut Muffins

2 c flour
1 t salt
2 t baking powder
⅓ c sugar
½ c crushed pineapple, drained
½ c chopped nuts
1 egg, beaten
½ c milk
¼ c vegetable oil

Combine first 4 ingredients in a medium mixing bowl. Add pineapple and nuts. Stir in egg, milk and oil mixing just enough to dampen dry ingredients. Bake in greased muffin tins at 400° for 20 - 25 min.

Yield: 12 - 14 muffins

Quick Coconut Muffins

1 18½ oz yellow cake mix
½ c margarine, softened
⅔ c water
3 eggs
1 8 oz crushed pineapple, drained
1 c flaked coconut
1 c chopped pecans
2 t coconut extract

In a mixing bowl, beat the cake mix and butter. Add the remaining ingredients. Fill greased or paper-lined muffin cups ½ full. Bake at 350° for 20 - 25 min. or until a toothpick comes out clean. Cool for 5 min. before removing from pans to wire rack.
Yield: 2 doz.

Raisin Sweet Potato Bread

2 c self-rising flour
2 c sugar
3 t cinnamon
½ t nutmeg
¼ t cloves
1½ c mashed cooked sweet potatoes
1 c vegetable oil
3 eggs
3 t vanilla extract
¼ c raisins

Combine first 5 ingredients. Combine potatoes, oil, eggs and vanilla. Stir into dry ingredients just until moistened. Fold in raisins. Pour into 2 greased 8 x 4 x 2 in loaf pans. Bake in 350° oven for 55 - 60 min. or until toothpick comes out clean. Cool 10 min before removing from pans to wire racks.

Robert Reed's mother's Zucchini Nut Bread

3 eggs – beat until fluffy
1 c salad oil
2 c sugar
3 c grated zucchini
1 T vanilla
3 c sifted flour
1 t soda
1 t salt
½ t baking powder
2 t vanilla extract
¼ c nuts

Mix and bake in 2 greased and floured 9 x 5 x 2 in loaf pans at 325° for about 45 min.

Murphy Boys at Christmas

Rosemary Cook's Pineapple Cherry Nut Bread

3 c sifted flour
4 t baking powder
¾ c sugar
1 t salt
1 c chopped nuts
½ c candied cherries, halved
1 egg
1 small can crushed pineapple
½ c milk
¼ c vegetable oil

Grease 9 x 5 x 3 in pan. Sift flour, baking powder, sugar and salt into a large bowl; stir in nuts and cherries. Beat egg well. Stir in pineapple and syrup, milk and vegetable oil. Add all at once to flour mixture. Stir just until evenly moist. Spoon into prepared pan. Spread top even.
Bake 350° 1 hr. 15 min. Test with wooden pick. Cool on rack until completely cool. Store overnight to mellow flavors and make slicing easier.

Salem Tavern Muffins

1 16 oz can pumpkin
2 T melted butter
4 eggs
1 1/4 c flour
2 c sugar
1 1/2 T baking powder
3/4 T nutmeg
3/4 T cinnamon
1/2 c milk
1 c raisins
1 T vanilla extract
1 t salt

Mix dry ingredients. Mix wet ingredients except milk. Blend dry ingredients with wet and slowly add milk, stirring constantly. Add raisins and vanilla and mix. Pour batter into greased muffin tins and bake in a 375° oven until golden.

Makes about 2 doz. muffins

Savory Cheddar Bread

2 c flour
4 t baking powder
1 T sugar
½ t onion salt
½ t dried oregano
¼ t ground mustard
1¼ c shredded sharp cheddar cheese
1 egg, well-beaten
1 c milk
1 T butter, melted

Combine first 7 ingredients in a bowl and set aside. Combine egg, milk and butter. Add all at once to dry ingredients, stir just until moistened. Spread batter in a greased 8½ x 4½ in loaf pan. Bake 350° for 45 min.

Yield: 1 loaf

Self-rising Flour Substitute

As a substitute for each cup of self-rising flour, place 1½ t baking powder and ½ t salt in a measuring cup. Add all purpose flour to equal one cup.

Heloise's Homemade Baking Mix

8 c flour
⅓ c baking powder
2 t salt
8 t sugar (optional)
1 c shortening
⅓ c milk for each cup of mix

Mix all dry ingredients together in a large bowl. Using a pastry blender, cut in the shortening until the mixture resembles coarse meal. Store in tightly covered container, preferably in refrigerator. To make biscuits, use ⅓ c milk for each c of mix. Bake 450° for 12-15 min.

Sour Cream Coffee Cake

1 c butter, softened	1/8 t salt
2 c sugar	1 t baking powder
2 eggs	1/3 c flour
1 c sour cream	1/2 c brown sugar
1/2 t vanilla	2 T melted butter
2 c flour	1 t cinnamon

Preheat oven to 350°. Grease 9 X 13 pan. Cream 1 c butter and sugar. Add eggs, sour cream and vanilla. Add 2 c flour, baking powder and salt. Spread 1/2 of batter in pan. Mix together 1/3 c flour, brown sugar, 2 T melted butter and cinnamon. Sprinkle cake batter with 1/2 of filling. Spread second half of batter over filling, then sprinkle remaining filling on top. Bake 35 - 40 min.

18 servings

Spiced Zucchini Bread

- 3 c flour
- 2 t soda
- 1 t salt
- 1/2 t baking powder
- 1 1/2 t cinnamon
- 3/4 c chopped nuts
- 3 eggs
- 2 c sugar
- 1 c vegetable oil
- 2 t vanilla extract
- 2 c shredded zucchini
- 1 8oz crushed pineapple, drained

Combine first 6 ingredients; set aside. Beat eggs lightly in large mixing bowl; add sugar, oil and vanilla; beat until creamy. Stir in zucchini and pineapple. Add dry ingredients, stirring only until moistened. Spoon batter into 2 well-greased 9 X 5 X 3 in. loaf pans. Bake at 350° for 1 hour or until done. Cool 10 min before removing from pans; turn out on rack and cool completely.

Yield: 2 loaves

Surprise Muffins

1 egg
½ c milk
¼ c salad oil
1½ c flour
½ c sugar
1 T baking powder
½ t salt
Jelly, marmalade or preserves

Grease 12 muffin cups or use baking cups. Beat egg in milk and oil. Mix in remaining ingredients to moisten. Batter will be lumpy. Fill cups ½ full; drop 1 t jelly, marmalade or preserves in center of each and add batter to fill each ⅔ full. Bake 400° oven 15-20 min. until lightly browned.

Sweet Beer Bread

3 c self-rising flour
½ c sugar
1 12 oz beer
¼ c butter, melted

Stir together first 3 ingredients. Pour into a lightly greased 9 x 5 in. loaf pan. Bake at 350° for 45 min. Pour melted butter over top. Bake 10 more min.

Makes 1 loaf

Cheddar-chive Beer Bread

Add ¾ c shredded sharp Cheddar cheese and 2 T chopped chives to dry ingredients. Proceed as directed.

Tiny Cinnamon Rolls

1 8oz crescent rolls
1½ t sugar
½ t cinnamon
⅓ c powdered sugar
1 t milk
1 drop vanilla extract

Unroll dough and separate into 4 rectangles; pinch seams to seal. Stir together sugar and cinnamon and sprinkle evenly over rectangles. Roll up, jellyroll fashion, starting with a long side; press edges to seal. Cut each log into 5 slices and place in a lightly greased 8 in round cake pan. Bake at 350° for 12 min. Stir together powdered sugar, milk and vanilla in a small bowl until smooth. Drizzle over warm rolls.

Yield: 20 rolls

Williamsburg Sweet Potato Muffins

½ c margarine
1¼ c sugar
1¼ c sweet potatoes, cooked and mashed
2 eggs
1½ c flour
2 t baking powder
¼ t nutmeg
¼ t salt
1 c milk
¼ c chopped nuts
½ c raisins, chopped (dredge in flour first)
cinnamon sugar

All ingredients must be at room temperature. Cream margarine, sugar and sweet potatoes until smooth; add eggs and blend well. Sift together flour, baking powder, nutmeg and salt into a bowl; add alternately with milk to creamed mixture. Do not over mix. Fold in nuts and raisins. Pour into greased muffin cups ⅔ full. Sprinkle cinnamon sugar on top. Bake at 400° for 22-25 min.
Yield: about 2 doz.

Winkler Bakery Moravian Lovefeast Buns

1 c mashed potatoes (hot and mashed with no
liquid or seasonings)
½ c milk (room temperature)
1 c sugar
½ c margarine
2 eggs, beaten
2 packages yeast
½ c warm potato water
4 T orange juice
4 t lemon juice
1 t mace
½ t nutmeg
Flour (enough for soft dough)

Cream butter and sugar. Add potatoes
and mix well. Add milk and eggs. Mix well.
Dissolve yeast in warm potato water
and add to butter mixture. Combine
the flavorings and seasonings and add
to mixture. Add enough flour to
make a soft dough (it will be
sticky) Knead about 8 min on a
well-floured board. Place in
a greased bowl and cover with

a clean cloth. Let rise in a
warm place until doubled in size.
Punch down and let rest 5-10 min.
Flour hands well. Form dough
into small buns, placing on
a greased cookie sheet (not
touching) Slash top of each
bun with a razor blade to
release air (^). Cover and
let rise until doubled in
size. Bake 350° until
golden brown, about 15-20
min.

Terry Murphy

Yeast Biscuits

5 c self-rising flour
2/3 c Crisco
1/4 c sugar
2 c buttermilk
1 pk. dry yeast dissolved in 2 T
           warm water

Mix flour, sugar and Crisco together. Add yeast and buttermilk. Knead as biscuits. Cover. Put in refrigerator and use as needed. Bake 400° until golden brown.

Yellow Squash Muffins

1 lb yellow squash cut into 1 in slices
½ c butter, melted
1 egg, lightly beaten
1½ c flour
½ c sugar
2½ t baking powder
½ t salt

Place 1 in water in a saucepan; all squash. Bring to boil. Reduce heat; cover and simmer 5 min or until tender. Drain and mash; stir in butter and egg. In a bowl, combine flour, sugar, baking powder and salt; stir in squash mixture just until moistened. Fill greased muffin cups ¾ full. Bake at 375° for 20-25 min or until a toothpick comes out clean. Cool for 5 min. before removing from pan to a wire rack.

Yield: 1 doz.

Yummy Yeast Rolls

2 - 2½ c flour
3 T sugar
1 pack quick-rise yeast
½ t salt
¾ c warm water (120° - 130°)
2 T butter, melted

In a large bowl, combine 1½ c flour, sugar, yeast and salt. Add the water and butter; beat on medium speed 3 min. or until smooth. Stir in enough remaining flour to form a soft dough. Turn onto a well-floured surface; knead until smooth and elastic, about 4-6 min. Cover and let rest for 10 min. Roll dough to ³⁄₈ in thickness; cut with a floured 2½ in biscuit cutter. Place 2 in. apart on a greased baking sheet. Cover and let rise until doubled, about 30 min. Bake 375° for 11-14 min. or until lightly browned. Remove to wire rack.
Yield; 1 doz.

Cakes

A and P Grocery Spanish Bar Cake

½ c raisins
½ c water
1 stick margarine
2/3 c sugar
1 c flour

½ t baking soda
½ t cinnamon
½ t nutmeg
¼ T cloves
1 egg

cream cheese icing

Preheat oven 350°. Grease 9 in. square pan.
Simmer raisins in water until soft and
plump. Drain. Save 2 T liquid to use later.
Melt margarine. Remove from heat and
add sugar and 2 T raisin water. Blend
well. Stir in flour, soda and spices.
Add egg and beat well. Lightly stir in
raisins until combined. Bake about 30 min.
Cool cake in pan 5 min. Remove and cool
thoroughly. When cool, frost.

Cream Cheese Icing
2 T cream cheese
3 T margarine, softened
1½ c powdered sugar

½ t vanilla
2-3 T milk

Combine first 4 ingredients. Beat in
milk 1 T at a time to make a thick,
spreadable icing.

Apple Cake

3 eggs, slightly beaten
1½ c sugar
1 c vegetable oil
1 T vanilla
3 c flour
1 t baking soda
1 t cinnamon
4 c peeled, cored and chopped apples
1 c chopped nuts
Topping 2 T sugar and ½ t cinnamon

Mix together first 4 ingredients. Add flour, soda and cinnamon. Add apples and nuts. Divide batter evenly between greased and floured loaf pans. Sprinkle on topping. Bake 325° for 1 hour. Cool in pan 10 min before inverting. Wrap warm cakes in aluminum foil.

Makes   2   9×5 loaves
3   8×3 loaves

Banana Cake

½ c butter
1½ c sugar
2 eggs
2 bananas (mashed)
2 c self-rising flour

1 t soda
4 T buttermilk
1 t vanilla
¾ c chopped nuts

Cream butter and sugar. Add eggs, well beaten. Stir in bananas, soda, buttermilk, flour and vanilla. Add nuts and mix well. Bake in layer pans at 350° until done.

Banana Frosting
¼ lb butter
1 lb powdered sugar
1 large banana mashed
1 c chopped pecans

Mix well and spread on cake.

81

Butter Pecan Elegance Cake

½ c mashed bananas
1 pkg (4 servings) butter pecan instant
   pudding and pie mix
1 pkg. yellow cake mix
4 eggs
1 c water
¼ c oil
½ c chopped pecans

Combine all ingredients in large
mixer bowl. Blend well, then beat
at medium speed 4 min. Pour into
greased and floured 10 in. tube pan.
Bake 350° for 50 min or until cake
tests done. Cool in pan 15 min.
Remove from pan and finish cooling
on rack.

Glaze

1 ½ c sifted powdered sugar
2-4 T milk

Combine ingredients until smooth.
Yields about ½ cup. If desired,
decorate with banana slices and pecan
halves

Caramel Icing

2 c brown sugar
½ c butter
½ c Carnation milk
1 t vanilla

Cook in saucepan over
medium heat for about
5-7 min. Cool and beat.
Can add nuts if desired.
Spread on cake.

Carolyn Phillips' Carrot Cake

1 c sugar	2 t baking powder
1 c oil	2 t cinnamon
4 eggs	1 t salt
2 t soda	1 c chopped pecans
2 c flour	3 c grated carrots

Mix sugar and salad oil. Add well-beaten eggs. Combine dry ingredients into mixture. Stir and mix until smooth. Add nuts and carrots. Bake at 325° in greased and floured tube pan until cake tests done. (Carolyn adds ½ c coconut and ¾ c raisins that have been dusted with flour. She omits the nuts.)

Frosting

1 8 oz cream cheese	1 box powdered sugar
1 t vanilla	1 stick margarine

Cream margarine and cream cheese. Add sugar. Blend well. Add vanilla and spread on cake. If frosting is too thick, add a little milk to thin.

Cherry Crunch Cake

1 1lb can cherry pie filling
1 #2 can crushed pineapple
1 box yellow cake mix
1½ sticks margarine, melted
1 c chopped nuts

Butter a 9 X 13 in baking dish. Spread cherry pie filling over bottom; top with undrained pineapple. Cover with dry cake mix Dribble melted margarine evenly over cake mix. Sprinkle with nuts. Bake in a 350° oven for 45 min. or until lightly browned.

Chocolate Bundt Cake

1 box fudge brownie mix
1 can caramel pecan frosting mix
1 c sour cream
2 eggs

Combine ingredients in a large bowl. Mix well and pour in greased and floured bundt pan. Bake 350° for 50 min. or until cake tests clean. Cool and remove from pan. Sprinkle with powdered sugar.

Chocolate Coconut Cake

1 chocolate cake mix with pudding
1 c sugar
1 c milk
24 large marshmallows
1 (14 oz) coconut

Frosting

1½ c sugar
1 c evaporated milk
½ c margarine

2 c semisweet chocolate chips
1 c chopped nuts

Mix cake as directed. Grease 2 9 x 13 in pans. Line bottom and sides of one pan with waxed paper; spray with cooking spray. Divide batter among pans. Bake 350° 15-20 min. Cool. Bring sugar and milk to a boil. Reduce heat to med and stir in marshmallows until smooth. Add coconut. Spread over cake in pan without waxed paper. Using paper to hold, remove second cake and carefully turn over and place on top of filling; Remove paper. In pan bring sugar, milk and butter to boil. Remove from heat; add chips and stir until smooth. Add nuts. Pour over cake; cool to room temperature. Chill overnight. Serves 16-20

Chocolate Covered Cherry Cake

1 pkg. devil's food cake mix
1 21 oz cherry pie filling
2 large eggs
1 t almond extract

Preheat oven 350°. Lightly mist 9X13 in pan with vegetable oil spray. Set pan aside.

Place all ingredients into a large mixing bowl and beat with electric mixer on low 1 min. Scrape down sides of bowl. Increase speed to medium and beat 2 min more. Batter should be thick and well blended. Pour batter into prepared pan. Smooth top with a spatula, Place pan in oven. Bake 30-35 min. Remove from oven and place on wire rack to cool.

Frost with favorite chocolate frosting.

Chocolate Pound Cake

½ lb butter
½ c shortening
3 c sugar
5 eggs
3 c sifted flour
¼ t salt
½ t baking powder
½ c cocoa
1¼ c milk
1 t vanilla

Cream butter and shortening with sugar. Add eggs one at a time and blend well after each. Sift together dry ingredients and add alternately with milk. Add vanilla. Pour batter into greased and floured tube pan. Bake in 325° oven 1 hour 25 min. or until the cake tests done.

Chocolate Pudding Cake

1 pkg. chocolate cake mix
1 pkg. instant chocolate pudding mix
4 eggs
3/4 c water
3/4 c oil

Combine all the ingredients and beat for 3 min. on medium speed of mixer. Pour into a well greased large tube pan. Bake in a 350° oven for one hour or until done.

Christel Crews' Date Nut Roll

45 Graham crackers
24 marshmallows — diced
1½ c chopped dates
3 c (or less) chopped pecans
1½ c heavy cream — not whipped
(May use orange juice instead.
Add gradually. May need only 1 c)

Roll Graham crackers to fine crumbs. Combine marshmallows, dates and nuts. Mix thoroughly with 2¾ c cracker crumbs. Add cream. Mix thoroughly. Shape into a roll about 3½ inches across. Roll in remaining crumbs. Wrap well in wax paper, chill. Cut in 3/4 inch slices.
12 servings

Cinnamon Apple Cake

2 c flour	2 eggs
2 t cinnamon	1 t vanilla
1½ t soda	3 c chopped apples, peeled
1 t salt	2 c sugar
¾ c oil	

Topping

⅓ c packed brown sugar	½ c coconut
⅓ c sugar	⅓ c chopped nuts
½ t cinnamon	

Combine first 4 ingredients. Add oil, eggs and vanilla. Mix well (batter will be thick) Toss apples with sugar; fold into batter. Spread in greased and floured 9 x 13 pan.

For topping, beat butter, sugars and cinnamon. Stir in coconut and nuts. Mix well. Sprinkle over batter. Bake 350° for 40-45 min or until cake tests done.

Serves 16 - 20

Crazy Cake

1 stick margarine
3 eggs
1 box white or yellow pudding cake mix
1 pkg. cream cheese
1 lb powdered sugar
1 t vanilla
1 c chopped nuts

Preheat oven 350°. Grease and flour 9 x 13 baking pan. Beat together margarine and 1 egg until smooth, mix in dry cake mix just until crumbly. Pat mixture down in pan and sprinkle with nuts. Beat together softened cream cheese, remaining 2 eggs, powdered sugar and vanilla. Pour over mixture already in pan. Bake in 350° oven for 30 - 35 min.

Cream of Coconut Cake

1 pkg. white cake mix   2 T oil
1 c water   ½ c cream of coconut
3 eggs

Preheat oven 350°. Grease and flour 9 X 13 in pan. Combine all ingredients and mix well for 4 min. Pour batter into prepared pan. Bake at 350° for 35 - 40 min. Remove cake from pan and let cool.

Frosting

1 16 oz can cream cheese creamy frosting
1 8 oz Cool Whip
1 14 oz bag sweetened flaked coconut, divided
10 oz cream of coconut (approximately)

Combine prepared frosting, Cool Whip and ½ of the coconut (about 2½ c) until smooth. Add enough cream of coconut to reach a desired spreading consistency. Spread frosting over cooled cake. Top with remaining coconut.

Brice, Brent and Baron

Dark Chocolate Cake

1½ c sugar   2¼ c flour
1⅓ c shortening   1 t soda
3 eggs   1 t salt
2½ squares unsweetened   1¼ c milk
    chocolate, melted

Cream sugar and shortening and beat
in eggs. Add melted chocolate. Stir dry
ingredients and add alternately with
milk to the shortening and egg mixture.
Pour batter into 2 9in greased pans and
bake for 30 min. at 375°. Frost.

Mervelous Icing
4 squares unsweetened chocolate
2 c powdered sugar
3 T water
1 t vanilla
1 egg
6 t margarine
Melt chocolate. Add sugar, water and
vanilla. Stir. Add egg and beat in
margarine. Spread on cake
layers.

Dorla Boyles Date Nut Cake

1 c hot water   1 t vanilla
1¼ c chopped dates   1½ c sifted flour
1 c sugar   1 t soda
¼ c shortening   ½ t salt
1 egg   ½ c chopped nuts

Pour hot water over dates; let stand
until cool. Cream together sugar,
shortening, egg and vanilla until light
and fluffy. Sift together flour,
soda and salt. Add to creamed
mixture alternately with date
mixture. Stir in nuts.
Pour batter into greased and
floured 9 X 5 X 3 in. loaf pan. Bake
350° for 50 -55 min.
or Pour batter into 9 X 13 X 2
pan. Bake 350° 25 -30 min.
Cool and sift powdered
sugar over top
or Pour glaze of powdered
sugar and water over top.

At the Mill

Dottie Shoaf's Pound Cake

2 sticks butter   5 eggs
½ c Crisco   1 t vanilla
3 c sugar   1 t lemon
3 c flour   ½ t baking powder
1 c milk

    Have ingredients room temperature

    Sift ½ t baking powder with 1 c flour to add last. Grease and flour tube pan. Cream butter, sugar and Crisco well. Add eggs 1 at a time. Beat after each. Add milk and flour alternately. Add cup of flour with baking powder last. Add flavoring and place in pan. Bake 1 hr 10 min at 350°. Start in cold oven. Do not open the oven until cake has baked 1 hr. Cool in pan 10 min.

Glaze
    Heat 2 T butter and 3 T milk until butter is melted. Add 1 t grated lemon rind, 3 T lemon juice and 2 c sifted powdered sugar. Add milk and butter mixture. Mix well. Pour over warm cake. Use knife to help spread glaze over sides.

Duff's Restaurant's Texas Tornado Cake

1½ c sugar
2 eggs
2 c flour
2 c fruit cocktail, undrained
2 t baking powder
1 t vanilla
¼ c brown sugar ⎫ Topping
1 c chopped nuts ⎭

　　　Mix all ingredients except
brown sugar and nuts together.
Blend well but do not whip.
Pour into a greased 9 X 13 in
pan. Sprinkle with brown
sugar and nuts. Bake at
325° for 40 - 50 min. or
until done.

Easy Coconut Cake

　　　Bake white or yellow cake
mix in 9 X 13 in pan.
　　　Punch holes all over the
cake and pour 8 oz coconut cream
all over it. Let it soak
down into the cake.
　　　Spread on 8 oz Cool Whip
as an icing and sprinkle
with a heavy layer of
flaked coconut.

Iris Womble's Easy "Fresh" Coconut Cake

Bake Duncan Hines Golden Butter Cake
mix in 3 layers.
While cake is baking, mix
1 pkg. 14 oz frozen coconut with
1½ c powdered sugar and 1½ c milk.
Boil until slightly thick.
　　　Put together while layers
and filling are hot.
　　　When cake cools, put in
refrigerator.

Easy Fudge Frosting

Combine in top of double boiler
 3 squares (2 oz) unsweetened chocolate
 ¼ c butter or margarine
Melt over hot water.

Put into small bowl of mixer
 2 c confectioner's sugar
 ⅛ t salt
 1 t vanilla
 ⅓ c hot milk or cream

Beat on mod. speed until blended. Then beat in chocolate mixture. Beat until thick enough to spread. More sugar or cream may be added to give desired consistency.
 Enough for two 8 x 8 pans.

Easy Lemon Pound Cake

1 pkg. Duncan Hines yellow cake mix
1 pkg lemon jello instant pudding mix
¾ c oil
¾ c water
1 T lemon extract
5 eggs

Put all ingredients into a large bowl and mix well. Bake in a greased and floured tube pan for an hour at 350°.

After cake has been removed from the pan and while it is still very hot, mix the juice of 2 lemons and 1 cup powdered sugar and pour over it. Keeps well for several days.

Eclair Cake

1 box Graham crackers
2 pkg. vanilla instant
    pudding mix (4 serve)
2 (1oz) pre-melted semi
    sweet choc.
2 t light corn syrup
½ pt. heavy whipping cream

3 T milk
2 t vanilla
1½ c powdered
    sugar

Butter 9x13 in pan. Cover bottom with a layer of crackers placed close together. Prepare pudding by directions; fold whipped cream into pudding. Layer ½ pudding-whipped cream mixture. Add a layer of crackers. Add remaining pudding mixture. Top with layer of crackers. Chill 2 hours.

Topping

Mix pre-melted chocolate that has been held under hot running water to soften, corn syrup, milk and vanilla. Blend in powdered sugar. Spread quickly over top layer of graham crackers. Chill for several hours or overnight.

Edna Carrell's Moist Oats Cake

1 c quick oats
1¼ c boiling water
1 c brown sugar
1 stick margarine
2 eggs

1⅓ c flour
1 t cinnamon
1 scant t soda
1 T vanilla

Icing

1 c brown sugar
4 T butter
½ c canned milk

1 c Angel Flake coconut
1 c chopped nuts

Soak oats in boiling water for 20 min. Cream margarine and sugar. Add eggs one at a time. Add oats and then the flour which has been sifted with soda and cinnamon. Add vanilla. Bake in 9x13 pan at 350° for 35 min.
Mix brown sugar, butter, milk, coconut and nuts. Do not cook. When cake is done, cover top with icing and run back in oven with just broiler heat and cook until topping is browned. Remove from oven and cool before serving. Freezes well.

Eva Newman's Fresh Apple Cake

3 eggs
1½ c oil   } Beat or mix well
2 c sugar

3 c flour
1 t salt   } Sift and
1 t soda   add to above
1 t cinnamon   mixture.

2 t vanilla   } Stir with
3 c apples peeled and cut fine   a big
1 c chopped pecans   spoon
1 c coconut (fresh, frozen orcanned) and add
                                       to above

Bake at 350° for 45 min to 1 hour
using tube pan. It usually
takes an hour. Test with
toothpick.

Florida Sour Cream Cake

3 c sifted flour   3 c sugar
¼ t soda   1 c dairy sour cream
2 sticks butter   6 eggs, separated

Sift flour. Measure and sift
twice more with soda added. Cream
butter and sugar thoroughly. Add
sour cream and beat well. Add
egg yolks one at a time and beat
well after each. Blend in flour
mixture. Beat egg whites stiff
and fold in. There is no flavoring
Mix the cake by hand. Turn the
batter into a large greased
and floured tube pan. Bake in
a 300° oven for 1½ hours or
until cake tests done.

Flossie's Mississippi Mud Cake

2 sticks margarine
⅓ c cocoa
2 c sugar
4 eggs, beaten
1½ c flour

Pinch salt
1 t vanilla
1½ c coconut
1 c chopped pecans
Miniature marshmallows

Preheat oven 350°. Grease and flour 9 X 13 in pan. Melt margarine and cocoa together in sauce pan. Remove from heat and stir in sugar and eggs. Add flour, salt and vanilla. Mix well. Add coconut and pecans. Pour into pan and bake 45 min. or until done. Remove from oven and cover hot cake with miniature marshmallows. Spread frosting over warm cake.

Frosting

½ stick margarine
⅓ c cocoa
1 box powdered sugar

½ c milk
1 t vanilla

Melt margarine with cocoa in a sauce pan. Add milk. Remove from heat and stir in vanilla. Beat in enough sugar until creamy and of spreading consistency.

Frances Storey's Apple Sauce Cake

1 c brown sugar
1 c white sugar
1 c melted butter
2 eggs
3 c apple sauce
4 c flour
1 c chopped nuts
1 t vanilla
1 t cloves
3 t cinnamon
4 t soda
1 c chopped dates
3/4 c chopped maraschino cherries
1/2 box raisins

Combine sugars and butter; add eggs and apple sauce. Sift flour, spices, and soda. Add apple sauce mixture. Add cherries, nuts, vanilla, dates and raisins. Bake in a large greased and floured tube pan in 325° oven for about 1½ hours.

Frances Storey's Pumpkin Cake

- ¼ c vegetable oil ⎫
- 4 eggs ⎪
- 2 c sugar ⎬ Mix
- 2 c pumpkin ⎭

Sift
- 2 c flour ⎫
- ½ t salt ⎪ Add to pumpkin
- 2 t soda ⎬ mixture and cook
- 2 t cinnamon ⎭ in 9 X 13 in. flat pan
  at 350° about
  30 - 35 minutes

Icing

- 8 oz cream cheese ⎫
- 1 stick butter ⎪ Beat well
- 2 t vanilla ⎬
- 1 lb. powdered sugar ⎭

This is enough for a layer cake. Half of this will do the flat pumpkin cake.

Frances Storey's Turtle Cake

1 box German chocolate cake mix
1 (14 oz) bag caramels
3/4 c butter
1 small can evaporated milk
1 c chocolate chips
1 c chopped pecans

Prepare cake batter by package directions. Pour half of batter into 9 X 13 pan. Bake 350° for 15 min. Meanwhile, melt caramels with butter and milk in pan over low heat. Stir constantly. Pour this over the hot half of baked cake. Top with chocolate chips and pecans. Then pour on the rest of the batter. Bake 350° for another 20 min.

Fresh Peach Pound Cake

1½ c vegetable oil
2 c sugar
2 t vanilla
3 eggs
3 c self-rising flour
3 med. to large peaches, peeled and chopped

Combine all ingredients and mix well. Spoon into a greased and lightly floured bundt pan. Bake 350° for 1 hour. Cool in pan 10 min. then invert on serving plate.
12 servings

George Washington Pound Cake

½ lb. butter
2 c sugar
5 large eggs
2 c cake flour
½ t vanilla
Pinch of salt
½ t almond extract

Grease and flour tube pan. Heat oven to 350°. Beat butter and sugar until light and fluffy. Add eggs one at a time beating well after each egg. Fold in cake flour. Add vanilla, salt and almond extract. Pour mixture into prepared pan. Bake 1¼ hr. Cool cake in pan for about 15 min. Run a table knife around edges to loosen as needed then turn out on a rack to cool completely!.

Brent, Baron and Brice

Ginny Burton's Coconut Cake

1 box Duncan Hines Butter Recipe Yellow Cake mix
1 stick margarine
2 eggs
1 large can crushed pineapple, undrained

Mix 3 min, only Bake in 9 x 11 pan
at 350° until cake tests done.

While cake is baking cook
1 stick margarine
½ c sugar
1 t vanilla
1 c chopped nuts
1 small can evaporated milk

Boil for 5-6 min. until slightly
thick. Pour over hot cake. When
cake is cool, top with a large
Cool Whip and sprinkle with
a package of thawed frozen
coconut.

Ginny Burton's Cream Cheese Icing

8 oz cream cheese (room temperature)
Box XXXX sugar
2 T margarine (room temperature)
little vanilla flavor
little lemon flavor
little almond flavor

Mix all together and spread.

Hershey's Buttercream Frosting

6 T butter or margarine, softened
2 ⅔ c powdered sugar
½ c cocoa
4 – 6 T milk
1 t vanilla

Beat butter; add powdered sugar and cocoa alternately with milk, beating to spreading consistency. Stir in vanilla.
Makes about 2 c frosting.

Hot Fudge Cake

1 (18.25 oz) devil's food mix without pudding
1 c sugar
¼ c cocoa
2 c hot water
1 t vanilla

Prepare cake by package directions. Pour into lightly greased 9 x 13 in pan. Stir together sugar and next 3 ingredients; pour over batter. (It will sink to the bottom of the pan) Do not stir. Bake at 350° for 45 min. Let stand 10 min. Serve with vanilla ice cream and chopped pecans.

Yield: 12-15 servings

Ida's Scotch Shortbread

1 c butter (not margarine)
½ c powdered sugar
2 c sifted flour

Cream butter and beat in sugar gradually. Mix well with flour. Put dough on baking sheet and pat into a circle ¼ in thick an 7 inches in diameter. Pinch edge and prick all over with a fork. Chill at least ½ hour. Bake 375° oven for 5 min. (Watch so it doesn't burn.)

Jane Reed's Fruit Cake

1 lb. candied cherries
1 lb. candied pineapple
1 lb pecans or
  1 lb chopped dates
1 lb nuts

} Chop

12 oz frozen coconut
3 cans Eagle Brand milk

Mix all together. Grease a large tube pan. Line with brown paper and grease paper. Pour batter in pan and bake at 250° for 2 hours and 15 min.

Jane Mendenhall's Raw Apple Cake

1½ c Wesson oil
2 c sugar
3 eggs
3 c flour
1 t soda
1 t salt
1 t cinnamon
1 t vanilla
3 c peeled, cubed apples
1 c chopped nuts

Mix oil, sugar and eggs. Add dry ingredients. Mix well. Fold in apples, nuts and vanilla. Bake in greased and floured tube pan at 325° for 1½ hours.

Jean Padgett's Earthquake Cake

Grease and flour 9 X 13 in. pan.

Mix 1 c ground pecans
    and 1 c coconut
Sprinkle on bottom of pan

Prepare one German chocolate cake mix according to directions on the box.

Pour cake mix over the pecans and coconut.

Mix 1 stick butter, 8 oz cream cheese and one box of powdered sugar.

Pour on top of cake.

Bake 350° for 45 min.

Jeannine's Pumpkin Roll

3 eggs   2 t cinnamon
1 c sugar   1 t ginger
2/3 c cooked pumpkin   1/2 t nutmeg
1 t lemon juice   1 t vanilla
3/4 c self rising flour
Filling
  1 c powdered sugar   1 t vanilla
  4 T margarine   1/2 c chopped nuts
  1 8 oz cream cheese

Beat eggs 5 min. Add sugar, pumpkin and lemon juice. Mix well. Mix flour with spices. Add to pumpkin mixture. Add vanilla. Mix well. Grease and cover with wax paper 10 X 15 jelly roll pan. Pour in mixture and bake 12-15 min at 375°. Turn out on wax paper which has been sprinkled with powdered sugar. Roll up with wax paper. Cool. Unroll. Fill with filling. Sprinkle with nuts. Roll up as a jelly roll. Refrigerate. Cut into slices. Freezes well.

Key Lime Pound Cake

1 c butter, softened	1/8 t salt
1/2 c shortening	1 c milk
3 c flour	1 t vanilla
1/2 t baking powder	1/4 c key lime juice
3 c sugar	Key lime glaze

Preheat oven 325°. Beat butter and shortening until creamy. Gradually add sugar. Beat until light and fluffy. Add eggs, one at a time beating after each just until blended. Stir together baking powder, flour and salt. Add to butter mixture alternately with milk, beginning and ending with flour. Beat just until blended after each addition. Stir in vanilla and lime juice. Pour batter into a greased and floured 10 in tube pan. Bake 325° for 1 hr 15 to 20 min or until cake tests done. Cool in pan 10–15 min. Remove to wire rack.

Brush immediately with key lime glaze and cool completely (1 hr.)

Glaze: 1 c XXX sugar, 2 T lime juice, 1 t vanilla

Whisk ingredients together until smooth. Use immediately.

Lillian Bennett "Good Cake"

Add in this order
  1 pkg. Duncan Hines White Cake Mix
  ¾ c oil
  ½ c sugar
  1 c sour cream
  4 eggs - put in one at a time
      and beat after each

Filling
  3 T brown sugar
  1 t cinnamon
  ¾ c chopped nuts

  Bake in greased and floured
tube pan. Put in ½ batter; add
½ filling. Add remaining batter
and top with remaining topping.
  Bake 1 hour at 350°
  Leave in pan 10 min before
removing.

Louise Turner's Sour Cream Pound Cake

  1 c butter   not margarine
  3 c sugar
  3 c flour
  ¼ t soda
  6 eggs
  ½ pt. sour cream
  1 t lemon flavor
  ¼ t salt

  Cream butter and sugar.
Add eggs one at a time. Beat
after each. Put soda and salt
in flour. Add alternately
with sour cream. Bake in
a greased and floured tube
pan 1½ hours at 300°.
Turn out at once.

Margie Darnell's Pineapple Cake

#2 can crushed pineapple
1 box butter cake mix

Use 9 x 13 pan.

Put pineapple in pan. Spread cake mix over pineapple. Cut up 1 stick of margarine and put over mix.

Bake 350° for about 30 min.

Mildred Park's Pound Cake

½ lb. butter
½ c crisco or 1 stick margarine
3 c sugar
3 c sifted flour
1 c milk
5 eggs
¼ t baking powder
½ t salt
½ t vanilla

Cream butter, crisco and sugar. Cream well. Add one egg at a time. Beat well after each. Add baking powder and salt. Add flour and milk to the batter using small amount of milk with each cup of flour. Beat well after adding each cup. Add vanilla. Bake at 300° for 1 hr. 20 min. or until cake tests done in a greased and floured tube pan.

Mint Cake

1 pkg. yellow cake mix
½ t mint extract, divided
1½ c cold milk
1 (3.9 oz) instant chocolate pudding mix
1 (8 oz) Cool Whip, thawed
4-5 drops green food coloring

Prepare cake as directed. Add ¼ t mint extract; beat well. Pour into a greased 9 X 13 in pan. Bake 350° for 25-30 min or until it tests done. Cool completely on wire rack.

In a bowl, whisk milk and pudding mix 2 min. Let stand 2 min or until soft-set. Using the end of a wooden spoon handle, poke 24 holes in cake. Spread pudding evenly over cake. Combine the Cool Whip, food coloring and remaining extract; spread over pudding. Cover and refrigerate at least 2 hours.

Yield: 15 servings

Mom Kite's Devil's Food Cake

1 c sugar
1 c butter   cream sugar and
5 eggs   butter. Add eggs
one at a time.

Cook
½ c sugar   Cook until all is
½ c milk   dissolved well. Add
½ c cocoa   to first mixture.

Add
½ c cold coffee with 1 t soda
(mix together)
Add
2 c flour with 1 t baking powder

Flavor with vanilla (1 t)

Bake in layers at 350° until
cake tests done. Ice with
favorite icing.

Mom Kite's Pound Cake

1½ c Crisco   cream together
3 c sugar
Add 6 eggs – one at a time.
Beat after each
Add 1 t vanilla flavoring
1 t lemon flavoring

Mix 1 t salt   add alternately.
3½ c flour   Begin and
end with
1 c milk   flour

Bake in greased and floured
tube pan at 350° for 1¼–1½ hours
Check after 1 hr. If it is
browning too fast, lower heat
to 325°.

This was my mom's
recipe.

Krites' 50th Anniversary

Mom Krites Sugar Cake

Will fill two cafeteria size tray pans

8 c flour
1¼ c sugar
½ c shortening
1 T salt
2 pkgs. yeast
(can add 2 eggs if you like)

Dissolve yeast in 2 c lukewarm water. Add to first ingredients. It will take about another cup of water to make a soft dough. Grease bowl, put dough in and let rise twice as big. Punch it down and pat it out in pans. Put lots of brown sugar all over it. Punch holes in dough with finger tips. Sprinkle with cinnamon. Dot with butter generously. Let it rise double again. Bake 325°-350° over until golden brown.

Mounds Cake

1 fudge cake mix with pudding
2 c sugar
1 14oz bag coconut
1 12oz chocolate chips
1½ c milk
24 large marshmallows
5 T butter

Bake cake in 9X13 pan. When cake is half done, begin cooking over low heat 1c sugar, marshmallows and coconut. Cook until melted together. When cake is done, spread mix over hot cake.

In saucepan, combine 1 c sugar, 1½ c milk and butter. Boil 1 min. Remove from heat. Stir in chocolate chips until melted. Spread on top of coconut mix. Cool.

Tastes like Mounds candy bars.

Mr. Blackwell's Apple Sauce Cake

1 c butter
2 c sugar
3 eggs
2 c apple sauce
1 t soda
3 c flour

1 t nutmeg
1 t cloves
1 t cinnamon
1 box raisins
1 c chopped nuts
1 lb. candied fruit

Cream butter and sugar.
Add beaten eggs
Add applesauce mixed with soda
Mix flour and spices
Save out a little flour to
    dredge fruit in
Add flour to batter
Add dredged fruit
Pour in greased tube pan
Bake 3 hours at 250°

His son was one of my students — way back!

Mrs. Jones' Carrot Cake

2 c sugar
2 c flour
1 c Wesson oil
3 egg yolks and whites (separated)
1½ T hot water
½ t salt
½ t soda
½ t nutmeg
½ t cinnamon
1½ c grated carrots
1 c chopped nuts

Sift dry ingredients. Add egg yolks, Wesson oil and hot water. Add carrots and nuts. Fold in beaten egg whites. Bake at 350° for 1 hr. or until cake tests done.

Mrs. Jones was the lunchroom manager at Brunson School.

Mrs. Jone's 7 Up Pound Cake

All ingredients must be room temperature

2 sticks margarine
½ c soft shortening
3 c sugar
5 eggs
3½ c flour
1 t salt
7 oz bottle of 7 Up (about 1 c)
1 t vanilla flavoring
1½ t lemon flavoring

Mix as any pound cake.
Bake 325° in greased and
floured tube pan for
1½ hours.

Krites Family

Murph's Aunt Algae's Brownie Cake

½ c butter
2 c sugar
4 oz chocolate
2 eggs
1½ c milk

2 c flour
2 t baking powder
2 t vanilla
1 c chopped nuts

Cream butter and sugar. Add melted chocolate and beaten eggs. Sift dry ingredients. Add alternately with milk. Add vanilla and nuts. Bake in a loaf pan at 350° for 45 min.

Frosting (uncooked)

1½ c powdered sugar
2 oz chocolate
½ c butter
1 egg
pinch salt
1 t lemon juice

Melt butter and chocolate. Add beaten egg, sugar, salt, lemon juice and vanilla. Mix thoroughly.

Orange Pound Cake

2 sticks butter or margarine
½ c shortening
3 c sugar
5 eggs - one at a time - beat after each
3 c flour
½ t baking powder
dash salt
1 c fresh orange juice
2 t grated orange peel

Mix as any pound cake.
Bake 1 hr - 1 ¼ hr in 350°
oven or until cake tests
done in a greased and
floured tube pan.

Pour on glaze of
    2 c powdered sugar
    ⅓ c plus 1 t fresh orange juice

Mix well.

Peach Cake

1 c butter	2 t soda
1½ c sugar	2 t cocoa
2 eggs	1 t each allspice
2 cups peeled sliced peaches	cinnamon and
2 c flour	cloves

Preheat oven 350°. Grease 9 x 13 in. pan.
Cream butter and sugar. Add eggs. Mix well.
Heat peaches over med. heat until they make
their own juice. Add peaches and juice to
creamed mixture. Sift all other ingredients
and add to creamed mixture. Pour
into prepared pan. Bake 30 min. or until
it tests done. Cool 15 min. then frost.

Brown Sugar Frosting

½ c melted butter	¼ c milk
1 c brown sugar	1¾ c powdered sugar

Add brown sugar to melted
butter. Boil over low heat 2 min., stirring
constantly. Add milk and bring back to a
boil while continuing to stir. Cool to luke
warm. Add sugar (more if needed) and
beat until smooth.

Peach Pound Cake

1 c butter (only)	¼ t soda
2 c sugar	¼ t salt
6 eggs	½ c sour cream
1 t almond	2 c diced fresh or
1 t vanilla	frozen peaches
3 c flour	

Cream butter and sugar until fluffy. Add eggs, one at a time. Beat after each. Beat in extracts. Combine flour, soda and salt; add to the batter alternately with sour cream. Fold in peaches.

Pour into greased and floured 10 in tube pan. Bake 350° for 50-70 min or until it tests done. Cool for 15 min before removing from pan to a wire rack to cool completely. Dust with powdered sugar if desired.

Yield: 12 - 16 servings

Pet's Mandarin Orange-Pineapple Cake

1 box yellow cake mix
2 T margarine
4 eggs
1 can mandarin oranges and juice
½ c salad oil

Mix ingredients together. Pour into greased and floured 9 x 13 in pan. (can also be baked in layers) Bake 350° until done.

Cool then add filling

Combine 1 large can crushed pineapple with juice, 1 box instant vanilla pudding mix and 1 large container of Cool Whip. Beat with mixer until well-combined. Spread on cake.

Store in refrigerator

Pillsbury Plus Double Fudge Fancifills

Filling	Base
8 oz cream cheese, softened	1 pkg. Pillsbury
2 T margarine	Devil's Food Cake
¼ c sugar	Mix
1 T cornstarch	3 eggs
1 egg	⅓ c oil
2 T milk	1 c water
½ t vanilla	

Heat oven 350°. Grease and flour 9x13in pan. Blend all filling ingredients. Beat at highest speed until smooth and creamy. Set aside. Blend cake mix, eggs, oil and water until moistened. Beat 2 min. at highest speed. Pour half of batter into pan. Pour cream cheese mixture over batter, spreading to cover. Pour remaining batter over cream cheese mixture. Bake at 350° for 45 to 55 minutes or until toothpick comes out clean. Cool completely. Frost with your favorite fudge frosting. Store in refrigerator.

Pineapple Pound Cake

½ c shortening
2 sticks butter
2 ¾ c sugar
6 eggs
3 c sifted flour

1 t baking powder
¼ c milk
1 t vanilla
¾ c undrained
crushed pineapple

Grease and flour tube pan. Cream shortening and 2 sticks butter. Gradually add sugar and beat until combined. Add eggs and beat well. Add rest of ingredients. Place in a cold oven and turn heat to 325°. Bake about 1 hr. 20 min or until cake tests done.

Glaze

Mix ½ stick melted butter with 1½ c powdered sugar and 1 c drained crushed pineapple until combined

Remove warm cake from pan and place on plate. Pour the glaze over the warm cake.

Pumpkin Crisp Cake

Mix together
  2 cups cooked or canned pumpkin
  1 c sugar
  1 c canned milk
  3 beaten eggs
  1½ - 2 t pumpkin pie spice

Pour into a 9 x 13 in. dish or pan
that has been sprayed or lined
with wax paper. Put on crumb
topping.

Topping
1 box yellow or spice cake mix
1 c chopped nuts
1-2 sticks melted margarine

Mix all ingredients well
and cover first layer. Bake
at 350° for 50 - 60 min. Cool
and turn out of pan. Cut
into squares and top with
whipped cream.

Pumpkin Spiced Buttercream

1 lb powdered sugar
1 ½ T pumpkin spice
1 c butter, room temperature
2 T heavy cream
2 t vanilla

Sift sugar and spice into a large bowl. With electric mixer, beat butter on med. until creamy, about 2 min. Reduce speed to low and gradually add the sugar mixture, alternately with cream. Mix in vanilla. Increase speed to high and beat until fluffy, about 2 min.

DIY Pumpkin Spice

3 T ground cinnamon
2 t ground ginger
2 t ground nutmeg

1 t ground allspice
1 t ground cloves

Mix well and store in an airtight container.

Red Velvet Cake

½ c shortening
1½ c sugar
2 eggs
1 oz. red food coloring
3 t white vinegar
1 t butter flavoring

1 t vanilla
2½ c cake flour
¼ c baking cocoa
1 t soda
1 t salt
1 c buttermilk

Frosting

1 8oz cream cheese
½ c butter, softened

3¾ c powdered sugar
3 t vanilla

Cream shortening and sugar. Add eggs, one at a time. Beat after each. Beat in food coloring, vinegar, butter flavoring and vanilla. Combine flour, cocoa, soda and salt. Add to creamed mixture alternately with buttermilk. Bake in 3 greased and floured 9 in pans at 350° for 20-25 min. or until cake tests done. Cool for 10 min. before removing to wire racks to cool completely.

In large bowl, combine frosting ingredients. Beat until smooth and creamy. Spread between layers and over top and sides of cake.

Yield: 12 servings

Refrigerator Cake

3 egg yolks
1 c sugar
1 stick margarine, melted
1 c crushed pineapple
1 c chopped pecans
1 c coconut
1 box vanilla wafers

Beat egg yolks. Mix in sugar and margarine. Fold in pineapple, pecans and coconut. Separately, crush small box of vanilla wafers. In flat pan with sides, make layer of wafers then a layer of mixture. Repeat. Refrigerate for at least four hours.

Ruth Bowman's Apple Cake

2 ½ lbs apples
Sugar
Vanilla
½ c butter
4 eggs, separated
1 c slivered almonds

Peel apples and boil until tender. Season to taste with sugar and vanilla and turn into a baking dish. Cream butter with ½ cup sugar. Add beaten egg yolks and almonds. Fold in stiffly beaten egg whites; spread over apples. Bake in a 350° oven for 45 min. Serve warm with cream.

Serves 6

Sock-It-to-Me-Cake

Cake
1 pkg. butter cake mix
1 c sour cream
½ c oil
¼ c water
4 eggs
¼ c sugar

Filling
1 c chopped pecans
2 T brown sugar
2 t cinnamon

Glaze
1 c powdered sugar and 2T milk

Preheat oven 375°, Grease and flour a 10 in tube pan. In mixing bowl make batter by combining cake mix, oil, sour cream, sugar, water and eggs. Beat on high speed for 2 min. Pour ½ of batter into tube pan. For filling, combine pecans, brown sugar and cinnamon and pour over batter. Pour remaining batter over filling, spreading to cover. Bake 45-55 min, until cake springs back when touched lightly. Cool 25 min. Remove from pan. Make glaze by combining sugar and milk. Drizzle over cake.

Sweet Tropical Loaves

1 pkg yellow cake mix
1 8oz crushed pineapple, undrained
1 c evaporated milk
2 eggs
½ t nutmeg
½ c flaked coconut

Glaze
1½ c powdered sugar
2 T milk
3 drops coconut extract
2 T coconut, toasted

Combine first 5 ingredients. Beat on low until moistened then on high 2 min. Stir in coconut. Pour into two greased 8 X 4 X 2 in. loaf pans. Bake at 325° for 45 - 50 min. or until a toothpick comes out clean. Cool for 10 min before removing from pans to cool completely.

For glaze, combine sugar and milk until smooth. Add extract. Drizzle over loaves. Sprinkle with coconut.

Yield: 2 loaves

Terry's Chocolate Butter Cream Icing

2 sticks butter
1 c Crisco
1 t vanilla
2 lb confectioner's sugar
1 c baking chocolate
3-5 T milk

Beat butter and Crisco until smooth. Then add chocolate. Add sugar ¼ at a time mixing well after each. Add vanilla and milk. Mix on high speed until creamy.

Texas Fudge Cake

Boil together 1 stick margarine
½ c shortening
1 c water
4 heaping T cocoa
In a separate bowl combine
2 c flour
2 c sugar
Pour chocolate mixture over sugar and flour. Mix
Beat and add to mixture 2 eggs
Add to mixture ½ c sour milk
1 t soda
1 t vanilla
Pour batter in 9 X 13 ungreased pan and bake at 350° for 30 min.
15 min after cake is in oven, make the fudge frosting. When cake is done, frost immediately.

Fudge Frosting
Boil together 1 stick margarine
6 T milk
4 heaping T cocoa
Mix together, then add a handful of chopped nuts. Add 1 c powdered sugar to mixture and beat. Pour over hot cake.
Makes 20 servings

Texas Sheet Cake

Bake 20 min at 400° in a large
greased 1½ × 8 in cookie sheet with
low sides or 2 large cake pans

Bring to a boil
- 2 sticks margarine
- 1 c water
- 4 T cocoa

While hot add
and beat well
- 2 c flour
- 2 c sugar
- ½ t salt

Add and beat well again
- 2 eggs
- ½ c sour cream
- 1 t soda

Frosting
Bring to boil
- 6 T milk
- 1 stick margarine
- 1 t vanilla

Then add
- 1 box powdered sugar

Beat well and pour over cake
while hot. Sprinkle nuts on top
of cake.

Tom Webb's Dr. Bird's Cake

Sift all together in large bowl
- 2 c flour
- 1 t cinnamon
- 1 t baking powder
- 1 t salt
- 2 c sugar

Add
- 1½ c oil
- 1 8 oz crushed pineapple
- ½ t vanilla
- 3 eggs
- 2 c diced bananas
- ½ c chopped nuts

Combine all ingredients. Mix well
until blended but do not beat.
Bake in greased and floured
tube pan for one hour at 350°.

Glaze
- ½ c brown sugar
- ¼ of a 6 oz can of frozen orange juice

Mix and heat until hot but
do not allow mixture to boil.
Remove from heat and spoon
glaze over cake.

Virginia Zigar's Ice Box Fruit Cake

1 lb. graham crackers
1 lb. seedless raisins
4 cups nuts, chopped
1 c milk
½ lb marshmallows

Roll crackers fine. Add raisins and nuts. Melt marshmallows in milk. Add to other ingredients. Line container with wax paper and press mixture down firmly. Leave in refrigerator for 24 hour

W W 11   War Cake

You will need 2 c hot water, 2 c brown sugar, 2 t shortening, ½ to ¾ c raisins, 1 t salt, 1 t cinnamon, 1 t cloves.

Mix all the ingredients together in a medium to large pot/pan and place it on the stove. Cook the mixture until it begins to bubble, then boil for 5 min. Next, let it cool completely and when the mixture is cold (this is important — the mixture must be COLD) Add 3 c flour and 1 t baking soda dissolved in a couple t of hot water. Mix well and put the mixture into a greased tube pan. Bake in a 350° - 375° oven for about 1 hour.

Candies and Nuts

Baked Popcorn Twist

½ c margarine, softened
½ c brown sugar
3 quarts popped popcorn
1 c mixed nuts or peanuts

Mix together margarine and brown sugar until smooth and creamy. Pour over popcorn and nuts. Mix well. Spread in greased 9 x 13 in baking dish. Bake at 200° for an hour stirring every 15 min.

Variation: Add pretzels instead of nuts or in addition to them.

Makes 3 quarts

Bavarian Mints

Melt over low heat until smooth and creamy.
  2 c milk chocolate chips
  1 sq. unsweetened chocolate
  2 T margarine
  1 can condensed milk

Stir in 6-8 drops peppermint oil.

Pour into buttered pan or drop by spoon onto waxed paper.

The Murphy Family, 1965

Beth Tartan's Fabulous Fudge

1 stick butter or margarine
1¾ c evaporated milk (14½ oz)
4½ c sugar
½ lb marshmallows
2 1oz squares unsweetened chocolate
12 oz semisweet chocolate morsels
3 4oz bars German sweet chocolate
1 t vanilla

In a large heavy pot, place butter,
milk, and sugar. Bring to boil stirring
constantly with a wooden spoon. Let
come to a full rolling boil, then set pot
off burner and turn burner off.
Immediately add marshmallows and
chocolates stirring rapidly and constantly
until all are melted and mixture is
smooth. Pour mixture as soon as
it is smooth into a buttered
jellyroll pan. (10 X 15 in) (It helps
to have another person to quickly
scrape out pot) Let stand
until firm; cut into 1 in. squares.
Makes about 5 lbs.

Betsy Wall's Toasted Pecans or Peanuts

3 c pecans
½ c margarine

Melt margarine and stir in nuts until they are coated. Bake in 200° oven for an hour, stirring after ½ hour. Sprinkle with salt when you take them out of the oven.

Bourbon Balls

Mix { 2 boxes powdered sugar
1 stick melted butter

Add ½ c bourbon or brandy
Mix well and shape into small balls. Put a piece of pecan in center of ball. Chill at least ½ hour.

Chocolate coating
6-8 oz. squares of unsweetened chocolate
⅛ cake wax
butter about size of a walnut

Melt over hot, not boiling, water. Dip balls with fork. Place on waxed paper covered pans. Chill. Store in covered containers in the refrigerator.

Brunson Uncooked Fudge

1½ lb XXXX sugar
¼ c cocoa
½ lb margarine
½ c + 1 T milk
¼ t salt
1¾ c peanut butter
4½ c rolled oats (oatmeal)
1 t vanilla

Mix sugar and butter well, then add other stuff.

Will make enough to fill a cafeteria size tray.

Can't Fail 5 Minute Fudge

Mix ⅔ c (small can) evaporated milk, 1⅔ c sugar and ½ t salt in saucepan over low heat. Heat to boiling; cook 5 min. stirring constantly. Remove from heat.
Add 1½ c diced marshmallows, 1½ c chocolate or caramel chips, 1 t vanilla and ½ c chopped nuts. Stir 1 - 2 min - or until marshmallows melt. Pour into buttered 9 in square pan or spoon into drops on waxed paper.

Cherry Almond Bark

1 lb white candy coating
3/4 c chopped candied cherries
1/2 c unblanched whole almonds

In a saucepan over medium-low heat, melt coating, stirring until smooth. Add cherries and almonds; mix well. Spread onto a foil-lined baking sheet. Refrigerate until firm. Break into pieces.

Yield: about 1 pound.

Chocolate Covered Peanuts

6 oz. semi-sweet chocolate bits
2 1/2 c roasted peanuts

Melt chocolate in top of double boiler over hot (not boiling) water. Add peanuts to melted chocolate and stir to coat. Turn out on waxed paper spreading so that peanuts are separated as much as possible. Allow to cool.

Chocolate Pretzel Rings

48-50 pretzel rings
48-50 milk chocolate kisses
1/4 c M and M's

Place the pretzels on a greased baking sheet; place a chocolate kiss in the center of each ring. Bake at 275° for 2-3 min. or until chocolate is softened. Remove from the oven. Place and M+M on each, pressing down slightly so chocolate fills the ring. Refrigerate for 5-10 min. or until chocolate is firm. Store at room temperature

Yield: About 4 doz.

Christmas Candies

3 T baking cocoa
1 can condensed milk
2 T butter
Finely chopped nuts or sprinkles

In a heavy saucepan, bring the cocoa, milk and butter to a boil, stirring constantly. Reduce heat to low; cook and stir until thickened. Transfer to a small bowl. Cover and refrigerate until chilled. Roll into 1 in. balls; roll in nuts or sprinkles. Store in refrigerator.

Makes about 2-2½ doz.

Cow Pies

2 c (12g) white chocolate chips
1 T shortening
½ c raisins
½ c chopped slivered almonds

In a double boiler over simmering water, melt the chocolate chips and shortening, stirring until smooth. Remove from the heat; stir in raisins and almonds. Drop by tablespoonfuls onto waxed paper. Chill until ready to serve.

Yield: 2 doz.

Cracker Jack

1 c brown sugar
½ c margarine
¼ c white corn syrup
¼ t baking soda
dash of salt
1 gallon popped popcorn

In saucepan, combine brown sugar, margarine and corn syrup. Cook for 4 minutes. Stir in baking soda and salt. While preparing syrup, warm popcorn in 200° oven. (Warming it makes it less stiff when mixing it with the syrup.) Pour mixture over warmed popcorn, stirring until well coated. Pour on greased baking sheets. Bake at 200° for 60 min. Take from oven and break apart.

Creamy Peppermint Patties

1 8oz cream cheese, softened
1 t peppermint extract
9 c confectioner's sugar
3/4 c milk chocolate chips
3/4 c semisweet chocolate chips
3 T shortening

In large bowl, beat cream cheese and extract until smooth. Gradually add sugar, beating well.

Shape into 1 in balls. Place on waxed-paper lined baking sheets. Flatten into patties. Cover and refrigerate for 1 hr. or until chilled.

In microwave, melt chips and shortening; stir until smooth. Cool slightly. Dip patties in melted chocolate, allowing excess to drip off. Place on waxed paper until set. Store in refrigerator.

Yield: 4 doz.

English Toffee #1

1 T + 2 c butter, softened, divided (only)
2 c sugar
1 T light corn syrup
¼ t salt
1 c milk chocolate chips
1 C chopped pecans

Grease 10 X 15 in baking sheet with 1 T butter; set aside. In heavy 3 qt saucepan, melt remaining butter. Add sugar, corn syrup and salt; cook and stir over med. heat until candy thermometer reads 295° (hard crack stage). Quickly pour into prepared pan. Let stand at room temperature until cool, about 1 hour.

In microwave, melt chocolate chips; spread over taffee. Sprinkle with pecans. Let stand for 1 hour. Break into bite size pieces. Store in airtight container at room temperature.

Yield: About 2 lbs.

English Toffee #2

1 c white sugar
1 c brown sugar
1 c corn syrup
1 c butter
1 c condensed milk
pinch salt

Place all in kettle and boil, stirring constantly. Cook to 245° - 248°. Pour into buttered pan and mark into squares when nearly cold. If harder toffee is desired, cook longer. Dip in chocolate or wrap in waxed paper.

Foolproof Chocolate Fudge

18 oz semisweet chocolate morsels
1 can condensed milk
Dash salt
1 ½ t vanilla
½ c chopped nuts (optional)

In heavy saucepan over low heat, melt morsels and milk. Remove from heat. Stir in remaining ingredients. Spread evenly into waxed paper lined 8 in square pan. Chill 2-3 hours or until firm. Turn fudge onto cutting board. Peel off paper and cut into squares. Store loosely covered at room temperature.

Fudgemallow Raisin Candy

1   12 oz semi-sweet chocolate chips
1 c   chunk style peanut butter
3 c   miniature marshmallows
¾ c   raisins

Melt chocolate chips with peanut butter in saucepan over low heat, stirring until smooth. Fold in marshmallows and raisins. Pour into foil-lined 8 in. square pan; chill until firm, cut into squares.

Makes about 2 doz.

Honey Candy Rolls

1 c   non-fat dry milk powder
1 c   peanut butter
1 c   honey
½ t   vanilla

Combine all ingredients; shape into rolls. Store in refrigerator. To serve, cut into 1 inch lengths.
If desired, additional chopped peanuts can be added to the ingredients above or could be used to coat the rolls.

Jan's Sugared Nuts

1 c sugar
¼ c water
1 t cinnamon
dash nutmeg

Mix together and heat until it reaches soft ball stage Remove from heat and cool a little.

Add

1 t vanilla
2 c nuts

Stir until syrup covers all of the nuts. Turn onto waxed paper and separate.

Katherine Dice's Pecans

1 egg white
3/4 c brown sugar
2 c pecan halves

Beat egg white. Add sugar and beat until stiff. Fold in pecans. Drop individually on greased cookie sheet. Bake 250° for 30 min. Turn off oven and let stand 30 min. longer.

Louise Bradshaw's Peanut Brittle

1½ c sugar
½ c white Karo syrup
¼ c cold water
2 c fresh peanuts
1 T soda
¼ t salt

Combine sugar, syrup and water. Bring to a rolling boil. Add peanuts slowly, keeping boil. Cook until peanuts turn brown (about 8-10 min) Remove from heat and add soda and salt. Stir well. Pour and spread on a well-greased cookie sheet. Let cool. Break up.

Louise Bradshaw's Chinese Treats

2 6oz butterscotch bits
1 3oz can chow mein noodles
1 small can peanuts

Melt bits in top of double boiler. Add nuts and noodles. Mix until coated. Drop on waxed paper. Let harden.

Louise Hunter's Decorated Mints

3 egg whites
2½ boxes powdered sugar
2T light corn syrup
1t mint extract or lesser oil
¼ t color

Have all ingredients at room temperature. Put all ingredients in and mix at low speed until soft. With spoon, stir in enough sugar to make a stiff batter — stiff enough to roll.

Roll out on XXXX sugared board. Cut in small shapes.

Decorate with some of the "dough" that has had water added to make it go through the decorating tube.

Can be made up to a week before serving.

Mamie Eisenhower's Million Dollar Fudge

2 c sugar
Pinch of salt
1 T butter
1 5.33 oz evaporated milk
1 c semi-sweet chocolate pieces
6 oz sweet baking chocolate cut into small pieces
1 jar marshmallow creme
1 c broken nuts

Butter an 8 x 8 in pan.

Into a 2 qt heavy saucepan add the sugar, salt, butter and milk. Cook over med.-high heat stirring constantly until mixture comes to a full boil.

Boil 5 min, stirring constantly. Remove from heat. Add chocolate and marshmallow creme; stir vigorously and speedily until chocolate is melted and the mixture is a uniform color.

At once stir in the nuts and pour into the prepared pan.

Makes about 2½ lbs.

Baron, Brice and Brent

145

Marshmallow Puffs

36 large marshmallows
1½ c semisweet chocolate chips
½ c chunky peanut butter
2 T butter or margarine

Line a 9 in. square pan with foil; butter the foil. Arrange marshmallows in pan. In a double boiler or microwave-safe bowl, melt chocolate chips, peanut butter and butter. Pour over the marshmallows. Chill completely. Cut between the marshmallows.

Yield: 3 doz.

Mildred Park's Mints For Molds

2 T margarine
2 T crisco
2 T warm water
1 T butter flavoring
8 - 10 drops of oil of peppermint
1½ lbs XXXX sugar

Mix all well. Knead until smooth. Place small amounts in molds.

May add few drops of food color if you like.

Millionaires

14 oz caramels, unwrapped
2 T milk
2 c chopped pecans
2 c semi-sweet chocolate chips

Combine caramels and milk in heavy saucepan. Cook over low heat until smooth, stirring often. Stir in pecans and drop by teaspoon onto buttered baking sheets. Let stand until firm.

Microwave chips in 1 qt. microwave-safe bowl on high power one minute or until melted, stirring once. Dip candies into melted chocolate allowing excess to drip; place on buttered baking sheets. Let stand until firm.

Makes 34

Minted Walnuts

1 c sugar
½ c white corn syrup
½ c water
1 t peppermint extract
10 large marshmallows
3 c walnuts

Cook together sugar, corn syrup and water to soft-ball stage. Remove from heat and add peppermint extract, marshmallows and walnuts. Mix well. Cool slightly and roll into balls. When cold, store in foil paper.

This candy remains good for a long time.

Yield: About 1 lb.

Mom Krites' Fudge

2 c white sugar
2 c brown sugar
1 c milk
4 T cocoa
4 T Karo syrup
¼ lb butter
vanilla flavoring

Mix everything together and bring to a boil. Let mixture boil until it comes to soft ball stage. Remove from heat and beat. Pour in buttered pan. Let set and then cut.

Mounds

1 can Eagle Brand milk
1 t vanilla
1 (14 oz) bag coconut
1 stick butter
1 box powdered sugar
1 (12 oz or 16 oz) chocolate chips

Mix first five ingredients and set in refrigerator for 20 minutes. Roll into small balls and return to refrigerator for 2 hours. Dip in chocolate that has had wax added to it.

Mrs. Abahazi's Mints for Molds

2 lb powdered sugar
1 8oz cream cheese at room temperature
¼ t peppermint oil or to taste

Mix sugar and cheese together with hands until mixture is as smooth as putty. It is messy at first. Add peppermint oil and knead. Divide into 3 or 4 portions and color with few drops of food coloring as desired. Knead in color.

Shape dough to make a small ball about ½ in. in diameter. Dip one side in granulated sugar. Press sugar side down in mold. Unmold at once. Place on waxed paper on baking sheet and place in refrigerator until set, then store in airtight containers. Place waxed paper between the layers. Makes 150 mints.

Can vary with lemon or other extracts, as desired.

Norma Graham's Seafoam Candy

3 c packed light brown sugar (1 lb = 2½ c)
¾ c water
1 T light corn syrup
2 egg whites
Pinch salt
1 t vanilla

Combine sugar, water and syrup. Stir over low heat until sugar is dissolved. Continue stirring until candy ~~boils~~ then place a candy thermometer into syrup.

Boil without stirring to 256° (hard ball stage). Meanwhile, beat egg whites and salt until stiff but not dry. Add hot syrup gradually. Continue beating until all syrup is added and candy is very stiff and loses its gloss — this takes about 10 min of beating with an electric mixer. Add vanilla. Drop from a buttered spoon onto waxed paper. This freezes well.

Ohio Buckeyes

3 lbs. powdered sugar
1 lb. butter
2 lb peanut butter
12 oz semi-sweet chocolate chips
2/3 slab paraffin

Mix sugar, butter and peanut butter. Form into 1 in balls. Chill in refrigerator overnight.

In a double boiler, melt the chocolate, then stir in paraffin until thoroughly blended. Using a wooden pick to hold each ball lower into the chocolate mixture leaving a small area at the top uncovered to form the "eye" of the buckeye. Place on waxed paper on cookie sheet to cool.

Makes about 200

Orange Balls

1 box crushed vanilla wafers
1 c powdered sugar
⅓ c melted margarine
1 c nuts, chopped fine
1 small can frozen orange juice,
                          thawed

Melt butter and stir in remaining ingredients. Roll into small balls and dip in powdered sugar. Store in refrigerator or freeze.

Orange Pecans

1 T grated orange rind
¼ c orange juice
½ c sugar
2 c pecans

Combine orange rind, juice and sugar in medium size saucepan. Bring to rapid boil. Add pecans. Stir constantly over high heat until all syrup is absorbed. Remove pan from heat. Stir until pecans have separated. Turn out on cookie sheet to cool.

Makes 2 cups

Peanut Butter Fudge

3 c sugar
3/4 c butter
2/3 c evaporated milk
7 oz jar marshmallow creme
12 oz pkg. (2 c) peanut butter morsels
1 t vanilla
3/4 c chopped salted peanuts

In heavy saucepan, combine sugar, butter and milk. Bring to full rolling boil over medium heat, stirring constantly. Boil 5 min. stirring constantly. Remove from heat. Add peanut butter morsels; stir until morsels melt and mixture is smooth. Add marshmallow creme and vanilla. Beat until well blended. Pour into foil-lined 9 x 13 in pan. Sprinkle with peanuts and press into fudge. Chill until firm.

Makes about 2½ lbs.

Peanut Butter Snowballs

1 c powdered sugar
½ c creamy peanut butter
3 T butter or margarine, softened
1 lb white candy wafers

In a mixing bowl, combine sugar, peanut butter and butter; mix well. Shape into 1 in. balls and place on a waxed paper lined cookie sheet. Chill for 30 min. or until firm. Meanwhile, melt the white coating in a double boiler or microwave safe bowl. Dip balls and place on waxed paper to harden.

Yield: 2 doz.

Pecan Millionaires

3 c pecan halves
1 14 oz pkg. caramels
4 2 oz squares chocolate almond bark

Arrange pecan halves in groups of 5 on lightly greased cookie sheet. Place an unwrapped caramel in the center of each pecan cluster. Bake at 325° for 8-10 min or until caramel melts. Lift with greased spatula onto wire rack to cool. Place almond bark in top of double boiler and bring the water to a boil. Reduce heat to low; cook until almond bark melts, stirring occasionally. Spread on top of clusters.

Makes 4 doz.

Peggy's Almond Bark Candy

1 lb almond bark
3 T peanut butter
½ c chopped salted peanuts
2 c Rice Krispies

Melt almond bark and peanut butter in double boiler over boiling water. Into melted ingredients, stir in peanuts and Rice Krispies. Mix well. Spread thinly on waxed paper. Let cool. Break or cut into pieces and store in airtight container.

Peggy's Coconut Bon Bons

1 can condensed milk
2 lbs. powdered sugar
¼ lb margarine
7 oz coconut
1 c chopped pecans

Mix ingredients, chill, then roll in small balls and chill again. Dip with toothpicks into chocolate. Melt 12 oz chocolate chips and ¾ block of parafin in top of double boiler.

Makes about 120

Peppermint Candy

1 box sifted powdered sugar
½ stick butter
½ stick margarine
¼ t peppermint oil

Mix with hands. Thin with milk but keep fairly stiff. Roll in small balls. Chill.

Chocolate Coating

1 small chocolate chips
1 small milk chocolate chips
½ stick parrafin (or less)

Melt in double boiler. Dip, using toothpicks, in hot mixture. Smooth over the toothpick hole.

Perky Pecans

1 lb. pecan halves
1 egg white
1 t cold water
½ c sugar
¼ t salt
½ t cinnamon

Beat egg white and water until frothy. Add pecans and coat well. Mix sugar, salt and cinnamon in a bowl. Add nuts and mix well. Bake in a buttered jelly roll pan at 225° for one hour, stirring every 15 min.

Pet's Fudge

5 c sugar
1 large can evaporated milk
2 sticks margarine
1 pt. marshmallow cream
18 oz. semisweet chocolate chips
1 T vanilla
1 c nuts

Bring to rolling boil – sugar, milk and margarine. Boil 8 min. stirring constantly. Remove from heat and add marshmallow cream, chocolate chips, vanilla and nuts. Beat until smooth and pour into a buttered pan.

(Makes a bunch.)

Quick Chocolate Nut Clusters

½ c butter
1 T vanilla
1 lb. confectioner's sugar
⅓ c cocoa
5 T evaporated milk
8 oz. broken nuts

Melt butter in large, heavy saucepan. Add everything except nuts. Cook, stirring constantly, just until the mixture starts to bubble around the edges. Remove from heat. Add nuts. Place tablespoonfuls of mixture on sheets of waxed paper and cool thoroughly.

Christmas Morning

Pulled Mints
(Do not make in wet or damp weather)

2 c sugar
1 c water
½ stick butter

Cook without stirring until thermometer reaches hard ball stage. Remove immediately and pour onto a marble slab that has been cooled with ice and then greased with butter. Have this ready so you can pour when temperature is reached Add 6-8 drops oil of peppermint and a few drops of cake color or leave white Grease hands with butter. Pull mix over from edges. It will be HOT. Work as quickly as you can. Begin to pull. Using finger tips as much as possible, pull until it loses its shine and you can hear it "knock" when it hits. Twist into small strands. Cut with scissors. Work quickly or it will get too hard. Store in air-tight tin to mellow.

Roasted Pecan Clusters

3 T margarine
3 c pecan pieces
12 oz chocolate candy coating wafers

Melt margarine in 15 X 10 in pan while oven heats to 300°. Spread pecans in pan, tossing to coat with margarine. Bake at 300° for 30 min, stirring twice.

Melt candy coating in heavy saucepan over low heat. Cool 2 min, add pecans and stir until coated. Drop by rounded teaspoons onto waxed paper. Cool. Peel from paper; store in an airtight container.

Rocky Road Clusters

Melt 6 oz (1 c) semisweet chocolate chips in top of double boiler set over simmering water.

Stir in 1 c each chopped pecans and mini marshmallows.

Drop by heaping tablespoons onto waxed paper.

Chill to set.

Russell Stover Candy

2½ sticks margarine
1 c Eagle Brand milk
5 c coconut
3 c confectioner's sugar
5 c pecans

Stir together margarine, milk and coconut. Add sugar and nuts. Chill and make into small balls. Roll in confectioner's sugar or dip in chocolate.

Salted Pecans

1 lb pecan halves
4 T butter, melted
salt

Place nuts in shallow pan in 200° oven. When nuts are warm, pour butter over them. Stir to coat. Salt to taste. Toast in oven for 4 hours, stirring occasionally so nuts don't become too brown on one side. Store in airtight container.

Make 2-2½ cups

Snowy White Fudge

1 c butter (2 sticks)
1 12 oz evaporated milk
4 c sugar
1 12 oz white candy making wafers
1 jar marshmallow creme
1 c chopped nuts
1 t vanilla

Let butter begin to melt in heavy 3 qt saucepan. Brush sides of pan with melted butter. Add milk and sugar. Cook over med. heat to boiling about 8 min, whisking constantly to dissolve sugar. Cook over med. heat, whisking frequently, to soft ball stage (236°) about 12-15 min. Remove from heat. Add candy wafers, marshmallow cream, nuts and vanilla; Stir until blended. Quickly pour into buttered 9 x 13 in. pan. When firm, cut into 1 in squares. Makes 117 pieces - about 4 lbs.

Spiced Peanuts

1 egg white
1½ c salted peanuts
½ c sugar
1 t cinnamon

Combine egg white with 1 t water and beat until frothy. Add peanuts and stir until nuts are well coated. Combine sugar and cinnamon; add to peanuts and mix well. Spread coated peanuts in oiled shallow baking pan. Bake in very slow (250°) oven, stirring every 20 min. for 1 hour or until coating hardens.

Makes 2 cups

Spiced Pecan Halves

1 c sugar
½ t cinnamon
⅓ c evaporated milk
2 c pecan halves
1 t vanilla

Boil sugar, cinnamon and evaporated milk to soft ball stage. Add pecan halves and vanilla. Using a sloted spoon, quickly drop pecans individually onto waxed paper.

Yield: 2 cups

Spiced Pecans

1 c sugar
2 t cinnamon
1 t salt
½ t nutmeg
¼ t cloves
¼ c water
3 c pecan halves, toasted

Combine first 6 ingredients in a saucepan. Cook over medium-low heat, stirring constantly until sugar is dissolved. Cook 9 more minutes on med.-low until it reaches 236° on a candy thermometer. Do not stir. Place pecans in large bowl; pour hot mixture over pecans. Stir until they start to lose their gloss. Spread pecans on waxed paper and seperate quickly with a fork. Cool completely. Store in airtight container.

Makes 3 cups

Strawberry Bon Bons

1 can Eagle Brand milk
1 7oz flaked coconut (5⅓ c)
1 6oz strawberry Jello
1 c ground blanched almonds
1 t almond extract
1½ t red food color

In bowl combine milk, coconut, ⅓ c Jello, almonds, extract and enough red color to tint mix a strawberry shade. Chill until firm enough to handle. Use ½ T to make into strawberry shapes. Sprinkle remaining Jello on wax paper; roll strawberries to coat. Place on wax-paper lined sheets and chill.

For stems

2¼ c sifted powdered sugar
3 T whipping cream
Green food color

Combine ingredients. Using pastry bag with open star tips, pipe small amount on top of each strawberry. Cover; store at room temperature or in refrigerator.

(Note: I use a little green plastic stem that can be bought at cake decorating stores. They look prettier and they are easy to do!)

163

Sugar Coated Peanuts

4 c peanuts
1 c sugar
½ c water

Cook together on med. high for about 5 min. Let peanuts soak up sugar and water.

Put on a cookie sheet and roast at 250° for about 1 hour. Stir about each 15 min.

Sugared Pecans

1 c sugar
5 T water
1 T cinnamon
pinch of salt
3-4 c pecans
1 T vanilla

In saucepan, mix together sugar, water, cinnamon and salt. Boil for 3 minutes. Stir in pecans. Boil 2 more minutes. Add vanilla. Stir until nuts are sugary. Pour onto waxed paper. Separate nuts with fork. Let dry and cool. Store in airtight container.

Makes 3-4 cups

Turtles

1. Put a pile of pecan pieces on some aluminum foil.
2. Melt caramel
3. Drop melted caramel by teaspoon onto nuts.
4. Let harden
5. Melt chocolate
6. Dip caramel and nuts in melted chocolate
7. Put into refrigerator to harden (15 - 20 min.)
8. Store in airtight container.

Uncooked Divinity

1 jar marshmallow creme
3 t water
2 c powdered sugar
1 c nuts

Whip marshmallow creme and water to stiff peaks with electric mixer. Fold in powdered sugar and nuts. Drop by teaspoon on waxed paper. Best the second day.

White Confetti Fudge

1½ lb white chocolate
1 can condensed milk
⅛ t salt
1 t vanilla
1 c chopped candied cherries

In heavy saucepan, melt chocolate and milk. Remove from heat. Add salt, vanilla and cherries. Spread evenly into waxed paper lined 8 x 8 in pan. Chill 2-3 hours or until firm. Turn fudge onto cutting board, peel off paper and cut into squares. Store loosely covered at room temperature.

Christmas Table at the Murphy's Home

Cookies

Acorn Candy Cookies

½ T canned chocolate frosting
24 milk chocolate kisses, unwrapped
24 mini vanilla wafers
24 butterscotch chips

Smear a dab of frosting onto bottom of a chocolate kiss, then press onto flat bottom of a vanilla wafer. Smear a tiny bit more frosting onto bottom of butterscotch chip and press onto rounded top of cookie. Repeat to make the other 23. Let cookies stand 30 min. for frosting to set.

Alice Johnson's Chocolate Cookies

1 box devil's food cake mix
⅓ c oil
2 eggs
10 oz or less Reeces peanut butter chips

Combine mix, eggs and oil. Batter will be stiff. Stir in chips. Roll into 1 inch balls. Place on lightly greased baking sheet. Flatten slightly. Bake 350° oven for 10 min. Cool 2 min. before removing from pan.

Makes 4 doz.

Ann Snelsire's Orange Cookies

1 box Duncan Hines orange cake mix
½ c oil
2 eggs

Mix all together. Make into
1 in balls. Bake 350° until
lightly browned. Cool
completely then ice.

Icing
2 T soft butter
confectioner's sugar
Tang – to taste – about 2 T
vanilla
milk to make the right consistency

Mix well and ice the
cooled cookies.

Betsy Wall's Corn Flake Chews

10 cups corn flakes
2 cups sugar
2 cups Karo syrup
2 cups peanut butter

Bring syrup, sugar and
peanut butter to a boil.
Add corn flakes. Drop by
T onto waxed paper.

Makes about 130 vanilla
wafer sized cookies

Big Brownie Oatmeal Drops

1 family size brownie mix with syrup
pouch prepared as directed on
box, using 2 eggs
1½ c uncooked oatmeal
1 c chopped nuts, optional

Heat oven to 350°. Lightly
grease cookie sheets.
Mix all ingredients until well
blended. Cover and let stand
30 min. for oats to absorb liquid.
Drop rounded T 1½ in. apart
on sheets.
Bake 10 - 12 min. until
tops look crackled and satiny.
Remove with spatula to wire
racks to cool.

Makes 32

Bon Bon Cookies

½ c soft butter
¾ c sifted powdered sugar
1 T vanilla
1½ c sifted flour
⅛ t salt

Heat oven to 350°. Mix butter, sugar and vanilla. Blend in flour and salt with hand. Add food coloring if desired. Wrap level T dough around filling. Bake 1 in apart on ungreased sheets for 12-15 min. until set but not brown. Dip tops of warm cookies in icing. Decorate

Chocolate Dough : Add 1 sq. unsweetened melted chocolate

Brown Sugar Dough : Use ½ c brown sugar instead of powdered sugar

Icing- 1c sifted powdered sugar, 2 T cream, 1 t vanilla. Add food color. For chocolate add 1 oz melted un- sweetened chocolate and ¼ c cream. For centers use cherries, dates, nuts etc.

Makes 20-25 cookies

Brunson Peanut Butter Cookies

8 dozen	4 dozen
1 c	½ c sugar
½ c	⅓ c brown sugar
2	1 stick margarine

Cream all together well

Beat well and add

2 t	1 t vanilla
2	1 egg
1 c	½ c peanut butter

Sift. Mix together and add

8 oz	4 oz flour
1 t	½ t soda
½ t	¼ t salt

Bake 375° for 8 minutes

Cherry Nut Nuggets

1 c shortening
1 3 oz cream cheese, softened
1 c sugar
1 egg
1 t almond extract
2 ½ c flour
½ t salt
¼ t soda
1 ⅓ c finely chopped pecans
Maraschino cherries, drained and halved

Cream shortening and cream cheese. Gradually add 1 c sugar. Beat until mixture is light and fluffy. Add egg and almond extract. Beat well. Combine flour, salt and soda. Stir into creamed mixture. Chill dough at least 1 hour.

Shape dough into 1 in balls. Roll in pecans and place on ungreased cookie sheets. Gently press a cherry half into center of each cookie. Bake at 350° for 16-18 minutes.

Yield: about 4 dozen

Chocolate Macaroons

1 can condensed milk
4 1 oz squares unsweetened chocolate
1/4 t salt
1 t vanilla
8 oz shredded coconut
1/2 c chopped nuts

Preheat oven to 350°. Generously grease 1 large cookie sheets. In top of double boiler combine milk, chocolate and salt.

Cook over hot, not boiling, water, stirring frequently until chocolate melts and mixture thickens, about 12 - 15 min. Remove from heat. Add vanilla, then coconut and nuts. Mix well. Drop by rounded teaspoonfuls, one inch apart, on cookie sheets. Bake 10 min. or just until cookies are set. Remove at once with spatula to sheet of waxed paper. Let cool.

Makes about 3 1/2 dozen

Chocolate Mallow Nut Bars

1 c semisweet chocolate chips
1 c butterscotch chips
1/2 c peanut butter
1/4 c butter or margarine
2 1/2 c miniature marshmallows
1 c salted peanuts

In microwave-safe bowl, combine the chips, peanut butter and butter. Cover and microwave on high for 1 min. Stir until smooth. Add marshmallows and peanuts; stir until well coated. Spread into a greased 13 x 9 in pan. Cover and chill for 30 min. or until firm. Cut into squares.

Yield: 4 dozen

Chocolate Mint Brownies

1 c flour	**Filling**
½ c margarine, softened	2 c powdered sugar
½ t salt	½ c soft margarine
4 eggs	1 T water
1 t vanilla	½ t mint extract
1 16 oz chocolate syrup	3 drops green food
1 c sugar	coloring

Topping

1 10 oz mint chocolate chips
9 T butter or margarine

Combine first 7 ingredients. Beat at medium speed 3 min. Pour into greased 9 x 13 pan. Bake 350° for 30 min. (Top will still look wet) Cool. Combine filling ingredients and beat until creamy. Spread over cooled brownies. Refrigerate until set. For topping, melt chocolate chips and butter over low heat in a small saucepan. Let cool for 30 min. or until lukewarm, stirring occasionally. Spread over filling. Chill before cutting. Store in refrigerator.

Yield: 5-6 dozen

Chocolate - Mint Creme Cookies

1½ c brown sugar
3/4 c butter, cubed
2 T water
12 oz semisweet choc. chips
2 eggs
3 c flour
1¼ t. soda
1 t salt

Filling
⅓ c butter, softened
3 c powdered sugar
3-4 T milk
⅛ t peppermint extract
Dash salt

Combine brown sugar, butter and water. Cook and stir over med. heat until sugar is dissolved. Remove from heat. Stir in chips until melted and smooth. Transfer to large mixing bowl; cool slightly.

Add eggs, one at a time. Beat after each. Combine flour, soda and salt; gradually add to chocolate mixture. Drop by rounded t onto greased baking sheets. Bake 350° for 8-10 min, or until set. Remove to wire racks; flatten slightly. Cool completely.

Combine filling ingredients; spread on bottom of half of the cookies. Top with remaining cookies. Store in the refrigerator.

Makes 4 dozen

Chocolate Mint Wafers

4 oz chocolate candy coating
1/8 - 1/4 t peppermint extract
18 - 24 vanilla wafers

Melt candy coating until smooth. Stir often. Stir in extract. Dip vanilla wafers in coating. Place on waxed paper until set. Store in an airtight container.

Yield about 1 1/2 doz.

Chocolate Nut Balls

2 c crushed graham crackers
  (about 32 squares)
2 c chopped pecans
1 16 oz can chocolate frosting
1 t vanilla
1 1/2 c powdered sugar

In a bowl, combine the first four ingredients. Shape into 1 in. balls; roll in sugar. Refrigerate for 1 hour before serving

Yield: about 5 dozen

Chocolate Oatmeal Sandwich Cookies

2½ + 2T margarine, softened
1½ c packed brown sugar
1 c sugar
2 eggs
4 t vanilla
2½ c unsifted flour
½ c cocoa
2 t soda
1 t salt
6 cups oats
12 oz semi-sweet chocolate chips
1 can condensed milk (14 oz)

Heat oven to 375°. Beat 1½ c margarine and sugars until fluffy. Beat in eggs and 3 t vanilla then combined flour, cocoa, soda and salt. Stir in oats. Drops by T on ungreased baking sheets. Bake 10 min. or until set. Cool. In saucepan, combine chips, milk, remaining 2 T margarine and 1 t vanilla. Over med. heat, cook and stir until chips melt. Immediately sandwich cookies together with chocolate mixture.

Golden Sandwich cookies: Omit cocoa. Increase flour to 3 cups. Proceed as above.

Chocolate Refrigerator Cookies

2 c flour
½ t baking powder
1 t cinnamon
¼ t salt
½ c butter, softened
⅔ c sugar
1 egg
¼ c chocolate syrup
¾ c chopped nuts

Combine first 4 ingredients, set aside. Cream butter and sugar until light and fluffy. Beat in egg and chocolate syrup. Stir in flour mixture. Shape into roll 2 in in diameter. Roll in the nuts. Wrap in waxed paper and chill several hours or overnight. Cut in ⅜ in slices. Place 1 inch apart on greased cookie sheets. Bake in preheated 350° oven 15 min. or until edges are lightly browned. Remove to rack to cool.

Makes 36

Walter Murphy

Chocolate Snowballs

1¼ c butter
⅔ c sugar
1 t vanilla
2 c sifted flour
¼ t salt
½ c cocoa
2 c finely chopped nuts

Cream butter and sugar. Add vanilla and dry ingredients that have been sifted together. Add nuts and mix well. Cover and chill well.

With hands, shape dough into 1 in. balls. Place on ungreased cookie sheet and bake at 350° for about 20 min.

Cool and coat well with sifted powdered sugar.

Chocolate Sugar Cookies

3 squares unsweetened chocolate
2 sticks margarine or butter
1 c sugar
1 egg
1 t vanilla
2 c flour
1 t baking soda
¼ t salt
Additional sugar

Melt chocolate and margarine until both are completely melted. Stir 1 c sugar into mixture until well blended. Stir in egg and vanilla until completely blended. Mix in flour, soda and salt. Refrigerate 30 min. Heat oven to 375°. Shape dough into 1 inch balls. Roll in sugar. Place 2 inches apart on ungreased cookie sheets. If thinner cookies are desired, flatten balls with bottom of drinking glass coated in sugar. Bake 8-10 min. or until set. Remove to wire racks to cool.

Cinnamon Sugar Cookies

1 c margarine
1 c granulated sugar
1 c powdered sugar
1 c vegetable oil
2 eggs
1 t vanilla
4⅓ c flour
1 t salt
1 t baking soda
1 t cinnamon
1 t cream of tartar
1 c chopped pecans, optional
colored sugar, optional

Cream butter, sugars and oil. Add eggs and vanilla; mix well. Add flour, salt, soda, cinnamon and cream of tartar. Stir in pecans, if desired. Roll into 1 in. balls. Place on greased baking sheets. Flatten with bottom of glass dipped in sugar. Sprinkle with colored sugar if desired. Bake 375° for 10-12 minutes.

Yield: 8 dozen

Cocoa Kisses

2 egg whites	3 T cocoa
¼ t cream of tartar	¾ t almond extract
⅛ t salt	⅓ c finely chopped
⅔ c sugar	almonds

Preheat oven to 200°. Line 2 large cookie sheets with foil. At high speed beat egg whites, cream of tartar and salt until soft peaks form. At high speed, beat in sugar 2 T at a time. Beat well after each addition. At low speed, beat in cocoa and almond extract until blended. Fold in almonds, reserving 1 T.

Drop mixture by slightly rounded T onto cookie sheets. Sprinkle tops with reserved almonds.

Bake 1 hr. 15 min. or until set. Cool on cookie sheets on wire racks 10 min. With metal spatula, carefully loosen and remove kisses from foil. Cool completely on wire racks. Store in tightly covered container.

Makes about 2 dozen

Coconut Bon Bons

1 can condensed milk
2 lb powdered sugar
¼ lb margarine
7 oz coconut
1 c chopped pecans

Mix ingredients; chill; then roll in small balls. and chill again. Dip with a toothpick into chocolate Melt 12 oz chocolate chips and ¾ block of paraffin in top of double boiler.

Makes about 120

Coconut Macaroons

⅓ c flour
2½ c flaked coconut
⅛ t salt
⅔ c condensed milk
1 t vanilla

Combine flour, coconut and salt. Add milk and vanilla; mix well. (batter will be stiff) Drop by tablespoonfuls 1 in. apart on a greased baking sheet. Bake 350° for 15-20 minutes or until golden brown. Remove to a wire rack to cool.

Yield: 1½ doz.

Congo Squares

Melt 1⅓ sticks margarine
Add 1 lb brown sugar
Beat in 3 eggs
Sift in 2¾ c flour
        1½ t baking powder
        ½ t salt
Add   1 t vanilla
        1 small bag chocolate chips
        ½ c chopped pecans

Bake in 7 x 11 in baking pan in 350° oven for 25 minutes. Cut into squares

Variation — Use lemon extract and butterscotch chips.

Cookies that taste like Heath Bars
(Rosemary Cook)

1 stick margarine
1 stick butter
½ c sugar

Bring to a boil and cook for 3 minutes.

Spread about 48 Graham crackers in a pan and pour this mixture over them. Sprinkle a few chopped-up nuts over this.

Bake in 275° oven for 10 min.

Remove from pan quickly.

Crisp Lemon Sugar Cookies

½ c butter or margarine, softened
½ c butter-flavored Crisco
1 c sugar
1 egg
1 T milk
2 t lemon extract
1 t vanilla
2½ c flour
¾ t salt
½ t soda
Additional sugar

Cream butter, Crisco and sugar. Beat in egg, milk and extracts. Combine flour, salt and soda; add gradually to creamed mixture.

Shape into 1 in. balls or drop by rounded t 2 in. apart on ungreased baking sheets. Flatten with a glass dipped in sugar. Bake at 400° for 9-11 min. or until edges are slightly browned. Immediately remove to wire racks to cool.

Yield: About 6½ dozen

Date Nut Balls

1 stick margarine
1 c brown sugar
½ lb. finely chopped dates
1 t vanilla
½ t salt
1 egg, beaten
2½ c Rice Krispies
½ c nuts
1 c coconut

In electric skillet on warm, melt and mix margarine and brown sugar, dates, vanilla and salt. Turn control to off and add well-beaten egg. Cook over low heat for 10 min., stirring often. Turn control to off. Add Rice Krispies and nuts. Let cool until mixture can be shaped with buttered hands into small balls. Roll in coconut or confectioner's sugar and place on waxed paper to cool.

Yield: 4 dozen

Delux Chocolate Marshmallow Bars

¾ c butter or margarine
1½ c sugar
3 eggs
1 t vanilla
1⅓ c flour
½ t baking powder
½ t salt
3 T cocoa
½ c chopped nuts
4 c miniature marshmallows

Topping
8 oz chocolate chips
3 T butter or margarine
1 c peanut butter
2 c Rice Krispies

Cream butter and sugar. Add eggs and vanilla. Beat until fluffy. Combine flour, baking powder, salt and cocoa; add to creamed mixture. Stir in nuts. Spread in greased jelly roll pan. Bake 350° for 15-18 min. Sprinkle marshmallows evenly over cake; return to oven 2-3 min. Using a knife dipped in water, spread evenly over cake. Cool. For topping combine chips, butter and peanut butter. Cook over low heat, stirring constantly, until melted and well blended. Remove from heat; stir in cereal. Spread over bars. Chill.
Yield: About 3 dozen

Duke Power Cracker Cookies

Cover cookie sheet with foil.
Use one with little sides.
Cover with 35 saltine crackers

Cook 2 sticks butter and
1 c sugar for 4 min.

Pour slowly over crackers.
Bake 400° for 4 minutes.
Sprinkle chocolate chips
over crackers. Bake 4
min. more.

5 Minute Chocolate Drop Cookies

12 oz chocolate chips
1 can condensed milk
1½ T butter
    Melt in a double boiler.

Stir into melted mixture
1 c flour
pinch salt
1 t vanilla
½ c chopped nuts

Drop in small balls on foil
covered cookie sheets. They do
not spread so place close
together. Bake 5 min. only
in 400° oven.

Makes 8 dozen

Forgotten Cookies

Turn on oven to 350°.

Beat 2 egg whites with a pinch of salt until very foamy.
Add ⅔ c sugar a little at a time and continue beating until very stiff.
Fold in 1 cup nuts and 1 cup chocolate or butterscotch bits (or ½ cup of each)
Drop on ungreased cookie sheet. (Covering the sheet with foil before dropping cookies will make the cookies solid on the bottom and easier to handle.)
Put cookie sheet in oven and turn off immediately.
Do not open door for 4 hours, or let them stay in the oven overnight.

Fruit Cake Cookies

½ c shortening
1 c brown sugar
1 egg
¼ c buttermilk
2 c flour
½ t baking powder
½ t soda
½ t salt
1 c chopped pecans
1 c chopped dates
1 c candied cherries cut in fourths.

Mix shortening, sugar and egg. Add buttermilk and sifted dry ingredients. Mix in nuts and fruits. Chill dough one hour. Drop by teaspoons about two inches apart on lightly greased baking sheet. Top each with a pecan half or half cherry. Bake 10 - 12 min in 400° oven.

Makes 4 dozen

Mixed fruits may be substituted for the cherries.

Ginger Cookies

1½ c shortening
2 c sugar
2 large eggs
½ c molasses
4 c flour
2 t baking soda
1 t cinnamon
1 t cloves
1 t ginger
sugar

Beat first 9 ingredients at medium speed with electric mixer until blended. Shape into 1 in balls and roll in sugar. Place on greased baking sheets and flatten slightly.

Bake at 375° for 8-10 min. Transfer cookies to wire racks to cool.

Yield: 7 dozen

Heloise's Cake Mix Cookies

Use your favorite cake mix but add only ½ c vegetable oil and 2 whole eggs.

You can add other ingredients as raisins, nuts or chips as to what you like. Mix well to remove any lumps and then drop the dough by teaspoonful about 2 in apart on an ungreased cookie sheet.

Preheat oven to 350°. Bake about 8-10 min and cool.

Holiday Coins

2 c flour
½ t salt
1½ sticks butter, softened
¾ c sugar
2 large egg yolks

1 t vanilla
½ c finely chopped nuts
3 T decorator's
   red sugar

Whisk together flour and salt. In another bowl, beat butter 1 min. Beat in sugar until fluffy. Beat in yolks and vanilla. Stir in flour mixture until dough comes together. Divide into quarters.

Roll each quarter into 6 in. log 1 in thick. Spread pecans and roll 2 logs in pecans to coat edge. Wrap in plastic and refrigerate 2 hrs or overnight. Repeat with red sugar and remaining 2 logs.

Heat oven to 350°. Unwrap logs. Cut each into 16 slices. Transfer to ungreased baking sheets.

Bake cookies 350° oven for about 14 min or until golden around the edges. Remove to wire rack. Cool completely. Store in airtight container.

Makes 6 dozen

Holiday Fruit Balls

1 lb graham cracker crumbs
1 lb candied cherries, chopped
1 lb candied pineapple, chopped
1 lb raisins
1 lb marshmallows
1 c evaporated milk (undiluted)
3 c chopped nuts
1 stick butter or margarine
coconut (may be tinted if desired)

Melt butter and marshmallows in the milk over low heat, stirring constantly. When mixture is smooth, pour over other ingredients (except coconut) and mix well. Form into small balls and roll in coconut. Store in refrigerator in covered container.

Makes about 200

Katherine Hepburn's Brownies

1 c unsalted butter
2 1oz unsweetened chocolate
2 eggs
1 c sugar
¼ t salt
1 t vanilla
½ c flour
1 c chopped nuts

Preheat oven to 350°. Spray 8×8 in pan with Pam. Melt butter and chocolate over low heat. Remove from heat. Beat eggs, sugar, salt and vanilla at medium speed until very light — about 5 min. Beat in chocolate mixture. Blend in flour. Fold in nuts. Spread in prepared pan. Bake in preheated 350° oven for 40 min; top will have shiny crust. Cool in pan on wire rack. Cut into squares.

Lemon Drops

1 stick butter, softened
½ c powdered sugar
3 T fresh lemon juice
1 t vanilla
1 ¼ c flour
½ c finely ground macadamia nuts
2 t fresh lemon zest
⅓ c powdered sugar (for coating)

Beat butter and ½ c sugar until creamy. Add lemon juice and vanilla. On low speed, beat in flour, nuts and zest (dough will be slightly stiff). Wrap in plastic and refrigerate 1 hour.

Heat oven to 325°. Pinch off heaping T of dough. Roll into balls. Place 1 to 2 inches apart on ungreased baking sheets.

Bake at 325° for 16–18 min. or until slightly browned near the bottoms of the cookies. Remove cookies to wire rack.

Sift ⅓ c powdered sugar over still warm cookies to coat. Repeat when cooled, if desired.   Makes 3 ½ dozen

Libby Reynolds   Pecan Puffs

4 sticks margarine
1 c powdered sugar
2 t vanilla
2 c chopped nuts
4 c sifted flour

Whip margarine and sugar until very creamy. Add vanilla. Stir in nuts and flour. Roll into small balls and bake at 350° about 15 min. or until light brown. Roll in powdered sugar while hot then again when they have cooled.

Makes about 100

Baron, Brent and Brice

Lou Maries Graham Cracker Delights

2 sticks margarine
1 egg, beaten
1 c sugar
½ c canned milk
1 heaping c graham cracker crumbs
1 c chopped pecans
1 c coconut
1 box graham crackers

Bring first 4 ingredients to a hard boil, stirring constantly. Remove from heat and stir in crumbs, nuts and coconut.

Place a layer of whole graham crackers on 10x15in. cookie sheet. Spread cooked filling on crackers and cover with another layer of whole crackers. Refrigerate until filling sets.

Icing: 2 c powdered sugar
¾ stick margarine, melted
2 T canned milk
1 t vanilla

Stir all ingredients until smooth. Spread on top of graham crackers and refrigerate until set. Cut in 1 in. squares. They freeze well.
Makes 96

Merry Christmas Cookies

1 c butter or margarine	2½ c flour
1½ c powdered sugar	1 t soda
1 egg	1 t cream of tartar
1½ t vanilla	1 t salt

Cream butter and sugar until light and fluffy. Add egg and vanilla and mix well. Stir together flour, soda and cream of tartar and salt and blend in. Mix well. Chill. Dough may be colored with food coloring before rolling if desired or roll and decorate with colored sugar.

Roll out on lightly floured board or between two pieces of waxed paper with the bottom one sprinkled with flour. Cut and place on lightly greased baking sheet. Bake in a 375° oven for 7-8 min. or until light brown.

Good!

Mint Sandwich Cookies

1 16 oz can vanilla frosting
½ t peppermint extract
3-5 drops green food color, optional
72 butter flavored crackers
1 lb chocolate candy coating,
        coarsely chopped

Combine the frosting and extract. Add food color if desired. Spread over half of the crackers; top with remaining crackers. Melt candy coating either in microwave or on stove until smooth. Dip the cookies in coating. Place on waxed paper until chocolate is completely set. Store in airtight container at room temperature.

Yield: 3 dozen

Mom Krites Moravian Cookies

1 qt. molasses
3/4 lb Crisco
3/4 lb brown sugar
4 T soda
3½ lb flour
2 T ginger
2 T mace
2 T cloves
2 T cinnamon
2 T nutmeg
2 T salt

Put molasses in a dishpan. Add Crisco and sugar. Stir to get all lumps out. Put in flavorings and salt. Put in about a cup of flour and soda. Stir real good. When that's all mixed up, add rest of flour. Knead well and when finished, put in a bowl with a piece of foil over it. Let stand overnight. Roll thin! Bake not over 250°. Makes about 6-7 lb cookies

No-Bake Cookies

6 oz chocolate chips
6 oz butterscotch chips
confectioner's sugar
½ c sour cream
¼ t grated orange rind
Pinch salt
2 c vanilla wafer crumbs

Over hot water, not boiling, in a double boiler, melt chips stirring to blend. Remove from heat and stir in ¾ c confectioner's sugar, sour cream, orange rind, salt and vanilla wafer crumbs. Chill until firm. Shape into small balls and roll in confectioner's sugar.

Oatmeal Sandwich Cookies

1½ c shortening
2⅔ c brown sugar
4 eggs
2 t vanilla
2 t cinnamon

2 ¼ c flour
½ t soda
1 t salt
½ t nutmeg
4 c old-fashioned oats

Filling: ¾ c shortening
3 c powdered sugar
7 oz marshmallow creme
1-3 T milk

Cream shortening and brown sugar. Add eggs, one at a time. Beat after each. Beat in vanilla. Combine flour, cinnamon, soda, salt and nutmeg; add to creamed mixture. Stir in oats. Drop by rounded t 2 inches apart on lightly greased sheets. Bake 350° for 10-12 min. Remove to racks to cool.

For filling, cream shortening, sugar, and marshmallow creme. Add enough milk to achieve spreading consistency. Spread filling on bottom of half of the cookies and top with remaining cookies.

Yield: About 4½ doz.

Old Fashioned Sugar Cookies

1 c oil
1 c butter or margarine
1 c granulated sugar
1 c powdered sugar
1 t soda
1 t salt
1 t cream of tartar
2 eggs
1 t vanilla
4 c flour

Cream oil, butter, both sugars, soda, cream of tarter and salt. Beat in eggs and vanilla. Stir in flour. Roll into small balls. Roll balls in sugar. Press down on lightly greased cookie sheet with a glass tumbler dipped in sugar. Bake in 375° oven about 12 min. or until lightly browned.
Makes 8 dozen

Note: Sometimes I need to add a little more flour. Also, the dough is easier to handle if chilled.   Good !!!

Orange Balls

1 box powdered sugar
1 12oz box vanilla wafers, crush
½ c chopped nuts
½ stick butter, melted
1 6oz can orange juice, thawed
Cookie Coconut

Mix all ingredients (except coconut) well and shape into small balls. Roll in cookie coconut. Store in refrigerator.

Makes about 5 dozen

Oreo Balls

1 package Oreos
8g cream cheese, softened
Chocolate wafers for coating

Crush Oreos and combine with the softened cream cheese. Roll into 1 in balls and chill until very cold. Dip into melted coating.

You can vary the kind of Oreos and the type of coating.

Peanut Blossom Cookies

1 can condensed milk
3/4 c creamy peanut butter
1 t vanilla
2 c buttermilk biscuit and baking mix
1/3 c sugar
1 9oz milk chocolate kisses

Stir together condensed milk, peanut butter and vanilla, stirring until smooth. Add biscuit mix and stir well.

Shape dough into 1 in. balls; roll in sugar and place on ungreased baking sheets. Make an indentation in center of each ball with thumb or spoon handle.

Bake 375° oven for 8-10 min. or until lightly browned. Remove cookies from oven and press a chocolate kiss in center of each cookie. Transfer to wire racks to cool completely.

Yield: 4 dozen

Peppermint Pinwheels

¾ c butter (only) softened
¾ c sugar
1 egg yolk
1 t vanilla
2 c flour
½ t baking powder
½ t salt
½ t peppermint extract
¼ t red liquid food color

Cream butter and sugar. Beat in egg yolk and vanilla. Combine flour, baking powder and salt. Gradually add to creamed mixture and mix well. Divide dough in half add extract and red color to one portion.

Roll out each portion between waxed paper into 16 x 10 rectangle. Remove paper. Place red rectangle over plain one; roll up tightly jelly roll style starting with a long side. Wrap in plastic wrap. Refrigerate overnight or until firm.

Unwrap and cut into ¼ in slices. Place 2 in apart on slightly greased sheets. Bake 350° 12-14 min or until set. Cool 2 min. Remove to racks to cool completely.

Makes about 4 dozen

Pet's Little Fruit Cakes

1 lb chopped pecans
1 lb candied pineapple, diced (all colors)
1 lb pitted dates, chopped
3/4 - 1 1/4 lb candied cherries, red and green chopped

Mix in big pan by hand.
Sift together
  3/4 c flour
  3/4 c sugar
  1/2 t salt
  1/2 t baking powder

Pour dry mixture over fruit being sure to coat all fruit.

Beat 3 egg until fluffy. Pour over mixture and mix together well. Pour into cupcake containers.
  Bake at 350° for about 30 min. for regular size cups and 20 min. for midget cups.
                    Good!

Pinwheel Cookies

	Filling
1 c margarine, softened	6 oz chocolate chips
3 oz cream cheese, softened	3 oz cream cheese, softened
1 c sugar	
1 egg	
1 T grated orange peel	½ c powdered sugar
1 t vanilla	¼ c orange juice
3½ c flour	
1 t salt	

Cream butter, cream cheese and sugar. Add egg, orange peel and vanilla; mix well. Combine flour and salt; add to creamed mixture and mix well. Cover and chill 4 hrs or until firm. Meanwhile, combine all filling ingredients in small saucepan. Cook and stir over low heat until smooth; set aside to cool. On floured surface, divide dough in half; roll each half into 12 x 10 rectangle. Spread with filling. Carefully roll up into a tight jelly roll and wrap in waxed paper. Chill overnight. Remove paper and cut into ¼ in slices. Place on ungreased sheets. Bake 375° for 8-10 min or till lightly browned. Cool on wire racks. Makes 8 dozen

Sandy Bosch's Christmas Mice

Start with an Oreo cookie (white iced ones are prettiest)

Dip a stemmed cherry in chocolate and attach to top of cookie for body. Unwrap Hershey kiss and attach two slivered almonds on back for ears. Attach the kiss to the cherry to make mousée face. Dot on two red eyes with gel frosting.

On the cookie, use some red and green gel to make a little holly decoration.

Santa's Sandwiches

1½ c flour
½ c cocoa
¾ t soda
¼ t salt
1 c sugar
1 stick butter, softened
1 egg
½ t vanilla
¼ t mint extract

Filling
2½ c sifted powdered sugar
½ C (1 stick) butter, soft
2 T milk
½ t mint extract
Red, green food coloring

Sift together flour, cocoa, soda and salt into bowl; set aside. In a large bowl, beat sugar and butter until smooth. Beat in eggs, then vanilla and mint. On low speed, beat flour mix into butter mix. Divide in half. Shape into logs 1½ in. in diameter. Wrap in plastic wrap. Refrigerate 4 hours. Heat oven to 375°. Cut logs into ⅛ in. slices and place on ungreased sheets. Bake 375° for 8-10 min or until almost firm. Transfer to racks to cool.

For filling beat sugar, butter, milk and mint until spreading consistency. Tint ½ green ½ red. Spread cookies with fillings and top with plain cookie. Chill   Makes 3 doz.

Scotish Fruit Balls

¼ lb butter
2 c powdered sugar
1 egg
¼ c chopped nuts
¼ c chopped dates
¼ c chopped marachino cherries
Graham cracker crumbs

Cream butter and sugar. Add egg. Beat well. Add fruits and nuts. Mix well. Refrigerate for 15-20 min. to make firm.

Put Graham cracker crumbs on waxed paper and roll little balls of mixture in them. Refrigerate until ready to serve.

Makes 32

Seven Layer Cookies

1 stick margarine, melted
1 c graham cracker crumbs
1 c coconut
6 oz chocolate chips
6 oz butterscotch chips
1 can condensed milk
1 c chopped nuts

Place in layers given in 9 X 13 in glass dish. Bake 350° for 30 min. Cut in squares when cool.

The Murphy Family

S'more Drops

4 c Golden Grahams cereal
1½ c miniature marshmallows
6 oz semi-sweet chocolate chips
⅓ c light corn syrup
1 T butter
½ t vanilla

Combine cereal and marshmallows. Set aside. Melt chips, corn syrup and butter until smooth, stir often.

Stir in vanilla. Pour over cereal mixture and mix well. Drop by T onto waxed paper lined baking sheets. Cool.

Yield: 2½ doz.

Summit Lemon Squares

Pastry
2 sticks softened butter
2 c flour
½ c powdered sugar
Mix and press out in a long pyrex dish. Bake 325° oven for 15 min.

Filling
4 eggs, beaten
Add 2 c sugar
6 T lemon juice
1 T flour
½ t baking powder
1 c chopped pecans
Mix and pour on top of pastry.
Bake at 325° for 40-50 min
Sprinkle with powdered sugar and cut into squares.

Toffy Bars

1 c butter
1 c brown sugar
1 egg yolk
2 c flour

Mix ingredients together. Press into an 18X13 in. pan — very thin. Bake 15 minutes at 350°.

Melt one large Baker's chocolate bar and pour over while warm. Sprinkle with chopped nuts. Cut into bars while still warm.

Desserts

Angel Lush with Pineapple

1 instant vanilla pudding mix
1 20oz crushed pineapple, undrained
1 c Cool Whip
1 10oz angel food cake

Mix pudding mix and pineapple. Gently stir in Cool Whip. Cut cake horizontally in 3 layers. Place bottom layer on serving plate. Spread 1½ c pudding mix on layer; cover with middle layer of cake. Spread 1 c pudding mix onto middle cake layer. Top with remaining cake layer. Spread with remaining pudding mix. Refrigerate for at least 1 hour.

Dessert can be decorated with small strawberries if desired.

Makes 10 servings

Banana Cream Dessert

4 medium firm bananas, sliced
½ c lemon juice
1 ½ c graham cracker crumbs (24 squares)
¼ c sugar
½ c butter or margarine, melted
1 (8 oz) sour cream
1 (3.4 oz) instant vanilla pudding mix
1 (12 oz) Cool Whip, thawed
⅓ c chopped pecans

Toss bananas with lemon juice; drain well and set aside. Combine the cracker crumbs, sugar and butter. Press into a 9 in. springform pan. Beat the sour cream and pudding mix on low speed for 2 min. Fold in bananas and Cool Whip. Pour into prepared crust. Chill up to 6 hours. Sprinkle with pecans.

Yield 8-10 servings

Butterscotch Pecan Dessert

½ c cold butter or margarine
1 c flour
¾ c chopped pecans, divided
1 (8 oz) cream cheese, softened
1 c powdered sugar
1 (8 oz) Cool Whip, thawed, divided
3 ½ c milk
2 (3.4 oz) instant butterscotch or
      vanilla pudding mix

Cut butter into flour until crumbly.
Stir in ½ c pecans. Press into 9 X 13 in
baking pan. Bake 350° for 20 min.
or until lightly browned. Cool. Beat
cream cheese and sugar until
fluffy. Fold in 1 c Cool Whip.
Spread over crust. Combine
milk and pudding mix until
smooth. pour over cream
cheese layer. Refrigerate 15-
20 min or until set. Top with
remaining Cool Whip and pecans.
Refrigerate 1-2 hours.
    Yield: 16-20 servings

Butterscotch Squares

1 stick butter
2 c light brown sugar
2 eggs
1 c flour

1 c chopped pecans
1 t vanilla
¼ t salt
1 t baking powder

Cream butter, sugar and vanilla. Add eggs, one at time. Beat after each. Put nuts in separate bowl and sift dry ingredients over them, mixing lightly to coat nuts well. Pour flour - nut mixture into creamed mixture and stir to mix well. Pour in 2 greased and floured 8 × 8 in pans and bake at 350° for 20 - 30 min or until done. Cool pans on rack before cutting into squares.

Cherry Meringue Dessert

6 egg whites
¾ t cream of tartar
2 t vanilla
2 c sugar
2 c crushed saltines (about 60 crackers)
½ c chopped pecans
1 8oz Cool Whip
1 20 oz cherry pie filling

Beat egg whites until foamy. Add cream of tartar and vanilla. Beat until soft peaks form. Beat in sugar 1 T at a time until stiff peaks form. Fold in saltines and pecans.

Transfer to a 9 X 13 in baking pan coated with non-stick spray. Bake 350° 20-25 min. or until lightly browned and edges begin to crack. Cool on wire rack. Spread Cool Whip over crust. Carefully spoon pie filling over top.

Serves 15

Chocolate Angel Food Dessert

12 oz chocolate chips
4 egg yolks, beaten
Pinch of salt
1 t vanilla
4 egg whites
2 T sugar
1 (8 oz) Cool Whip
1 c chopped pecans
1 angel food cake, sliced

Melt chocolate chips in top of double boiler over simmering water (do not let it boil). Slowly add beaten egg yolks to chocolate and stir well. Add salt and vanilla. Remove from heat. Beat egg whites stiff, add sugar and fold into chocolate mixture. Fold in Cool Whip and pecans. Set aside.

Line bottom of 9 x 13 in pan with ½ of cake slices. Pour chocolate mixture over layer and cover with remaining slices of cake. Chill 6 hours or longer. Top with Cool Whip if desired.

Yield: 12-16 servings

Chocolate Dream Dessert

Pastry

1 c flour   1 c chopped nuts

1 stick margarine

Mix all together well and spread in 9 X 13 pan. Press down mixture with a fork. Bake 350° for 20 min. Cool.

First layer

1 c powdered sugar   1 c Cool Whip

1 (8 oz) cream cheese   from large carton

Mix sugar, softened cream cheese and topping. Spread on baked pastry.

Second layer

1 (3½ oz) instant vanilla   2 c milk

     pudding mix   1 English

1 (3½ oz) instant chocolate   toffee or

     pudding mix   chocolate candy bar

Whip mixes with milk; spread on first layer. Spread with the remaining whipped topping. Sprinkle with grated candy bar. Chill.

Makes one 9 X 13 in. pan

Chocolate Ice Cream Pie

2 qts vanilla ice cream, melted
1 (5.9oz) instant chocolate pudding mix
2 10in graham cracker crusts

Whisk melted ice cream and pudding mix for 2 min. Pour into crusts. Freeze until firm. Pies may be frozen up to two months. Remove from freezer 10 min. before serving. Garnish with Cool Whip if desired.

Yield: 2 pies 6 -8 servings each

PTA Retirement Party

Chocolate Mint Freeze

1½ c cold milk
1 (3.9 oz) instant chocolate pudding mix
½ c miniature semisweet chocolate chips
1 c heavy whipping cream
¼ t peppermint extract

Whisk milk and pudding mix for 2 min.; let stand 2 min. or until soft-set. Stir in chocolate chips. In a small bowl, beat cream until it begins to thicken. Add peppermint extract; beat until soft peaks form. Fold into pudding.

Transfer to an ungreased 8 in. square dish. Cover and freeze for 2 hours or until firm. Remove from freezer 15 min. before cutting.

Yield: 9 servings

Coconut Angel Squares

1 8in angel food cake cut into ½ in. cubes
1½ c cold milk
2 (3.4z) instant coconut cream pudding mix
1 qt vanilla ice cream, softened
1 (8oz) Cool Whip, thawed
¼ c flaked coconut, toasted

Place cake cubes in a greased 9 x 13 in dish. Beat milk and pudding mix on low speed for 2 min. Add ice cream; beat on low just until combined. Spoon over cake cubes. Spread with Cool Whip; sprinkle with coconut. Cover and chill for at least 1 hour. Refrigerate leftovers.

Yield 12 - 15 servings

Coconut Balls

½ c sugar
¼ c butter
1 egg yolk
½ c chopped pecans

⅔ c crushed pineapple, drained
1 pkg frozen coconut
1 c heavy cream
1 box lemon wafer thins

Cream sugar and butter. Add beaten egg yolk, nuts and pineapple. Put 1 cookie on waxed paper. Spread with cream mixture, stacking until 4 cookies are used and there is a cookie on the bottom and one on top. Cover pan and chill 48 hours. Coat sides and top with whipped cream and sprinkle with coconut.

Makes 10 - 12

Can be frozen

Food For An Angel

35 crushed Ritz crackers
1 c chopped nuts
4 egg whites, beaten stiff
1 t vanilla
1 c sugar
Cool Whip
coconut

Mix crackers, nuts, beaten egg whites, vanilla and sugar. Spread in lightly greased 9 x 13 in pan. Bake 350° for 20-30 min. Cool. Top with Cool Whip and sprinkle (heavily) with coconut.
Let it mellow overnight in refrigerator.

Fresh Peach Crisp

1 c flour
1 c sugar
1 c brown sugar, packed
¼ t salt
½ t cinnamon
½ c margarine
4 c fresh peaches, sliced
1 T lemon juice
2 T water

Combine flour, sugars, salt and cinnamon; cut in margarine until coarse mixture. Combine peaches, lemon juice and water. Put in 9 x 9 in baking dish. Sprinkle flour mixture over peaches. Bake covered at 350° for 15 min. Uncover and bake 35-45 min. longer.

Serves 6

Lemon Delight

1 c margarine
1 c flour
3/4 c chopped nuts, divided
1 (8 oz) cream cheese, softened

1 c sifted powdered sugar
3 c Cool Whip, divided
2 instant lemon pudding mix
3 c milk

Cut margarine into flour until mixture resembles coarse meal; stir 1/2 c nuts into flour mixture. Press into a 9 X 13 in pan. Bake 350° for 15 min.

Combine cream cheese and powdered sugar; beat until fluffy. Fold 1 c Cool Whip into mixture and spread over crust. Chill.

Combine pudding mix and milk; beat 2 min. on low speed. Spread pudding over cream cheese layer. Spread remaining Cool Whip over pudding layer. Sprinkle with remaining nuts. Chill. Store in the refrigerator.

Yield: About 15 servings

Lillian Johnson's Good, Easy Dessert

Chocolate chip cookies
Milk
Cool Whip

In a container layer the ingredients.

Dip cookies in milk and make a layer.

Cover with Cool Whip

Make several layers and end up with Cool Whip.

Let stand in refrigerator overnight before serving.

Linda Dawson's Peach Cream Dessert

4 c peach slices
1 (14 oz) sweetened
  condensed milk
1 c cold water
1 (7 in) angel food cake

1 (3¾ oz) instant
  vanilla pudding
1 t almond extract
2 c Cool Whip

Cut cake into ½ in. slices. Arrange half on bottom of 9 x 13 in dish. Combine milk and water. Mix well. Add pudding and beat until blended. Chill 5 min. Add almond extract. Fold in Cool Whip. Pour ½ of cream mixture over cake. Arrange 2 c peaches on top. Repeat layers ending with peaches. Cut into squares to serve.
Makes 10 - 12 servings

Mint Chip Freeze

2 (14oz) pkg. Oreo cookies, crushed
½ c butter, melted
1 (12oz) canned milk
1 c sugar
½ c butter, cubed
2 (1oz) squares unsweetened baking chocolate
1 gal. mint chip ice cream, softened
1 (16oz) Cool Whip, thawed
Shaved chocolate

Combine cookie crumbs and butter. Press into 2 9X13 in dishes. Refrigerate 30 min. Combine milk, sugar, butter and chocolate. Cook and stir over med. heat until thickened and bubbly, about 12 min. Remove from heat. Cool completely.

Spread ice cream over each crust. Spoon cooled chocolate sauce on top; evenly spread to cover. Freeze until firm. Spread with Cool Whip. May be frozen up to 2 months. Remove from freezer 10 min. before cutting. Garnish with shaved chocolate.

Yield: Each pan 15-18 servings

Mom Murphy's Chess Tarts

1½ c packed brown sugar
2 eggs
1 T flour
2 T water
½ stick margarine
1 t vanilla

Cream butter, sugar and flour. Add eggs beaten with 1 T water. Add other T of water and vanilla to the mixture. Let stand a few minutes. Fill tart shells ⅔ full and top with chopped pecans. Bake at 375° for 30 min. or until done.

Makes 12 - 14 tarts

Party Bisque

Dissolve 1 pkg. lemon flavored jello in 1¼ c hot water; add ⅓ c honey, ⅛ t salt, 3 T lemon juice and 1 t grated lemon peel; mix thoroughly. Chill until partially set; beat fluffy. Whip 1 large can evaporated milk; fold into jello mixture. Spread 1 c vanilla wafer crumbs in bottom of a refrigerator tray; fill with jello mixture; sprinkle with 1 c vanilla wafer crumbs. Freeze until firm.

Serves 12

Pumpkin Crisp

Mix together well
  2 c cooked (canned) pumpkin
  1 c sugar
  1 c canned milk
  3 beaten eggs
  1½ - 2 t pumpkin pie spice
Pour into a 9 x 13 in. pan that has
been sprayed or lined with wax paper.

Put on crumb topping
  Mix together well
  1 box yellow or spice cake mix
  1 c chopped nuts
  1 - 2 sticks melted margarine
Pour over first mixture.
Bake at 350° 50 - 60 minutes.
Cool and turn out of pan.
Cut into squares and top
with whipped cream or
Cool Whip.

The Better-Than-Anything Dessert

First layer
1 c flour   1 c chopped nuts
1 stick butter
Mix together; press in 9 X 13 in pan.
Bake at 350° for 20 min.

Second layer
4 (oz) cream cheese at room temperature
1 c powdered sugar
1 (4 oz) Cool Whip
Combine and pour over first layer

Third layer
1 small instant vanilla pudding mix
1½ c milk
Combine and pour over second layer.

Fourth layer
1 small chocolate instant pudding mix
1½ c milk
Combine and pour over third layer

Fifth layer
4 oz Cool Whip
1 milk chocolate bar
Smooth Cool Whip over fourth layer
and sprinkle with grated chocolate bar.
Serve each piece with a marachino cherry.

Turtle Dessert

17 ice cream sandwiches
1 (12.25oz) jar caramel topping
1¼ c chopped pecans, toasted
1 (12oz) Cool Whip, thawed
¾ c hot fudge topping, heated

Place 8½ ice cream sandwiches in a 9x13 in dish. Spread evenly with caramel topping and sprinkle with 1 c pecans. Top with 2 c cool Whip and remaining ice cream sandwiches. Spread remaining Cool Whip evenly over sandwiches. Sprinkle with remaining ¼ c pecans. Cover and freeze at least 2 hours. Let stand 5 min. before serving. Cut into squares and drizzle with fudge topping.

Yield: 10 servings

"Wet Nuts" Ice Cream Topping

1 pint Karo syrup, blue or orange label
¼ t baking soda
½ c chopped nuts
3 drops vanilla

Boil the Karo five minutes rapidly. Add the soda. Cool a little and stir in nuts and vanilla.

Dressings

Barbecue Sauce

1 c ketchup
1 c water
2 t mustard
¼ t red pepper
1 T Worcestershire sauce
1 T vinegar
1 T chopped garlic

Combine all ingredients and mix well.

C.C. Pratts B-B-Q Sauce

For 3 broilers, combine
¼ lb butter or margarine
juice of 1 lemon
½ c vinegar
5 t salt
½ t black pepper
½ t red pepper

Mix all ingredients together. Mr. Pratt suggests increasing amounts of ingredients by about ⅓.

Cheese Sauce

2 T margarine
2 T flour
¼ t salt
1 c milk
1 c shredded sharp cheddar cheese

Melt margarine; blend in flour and salt. Add milk; cook and stir until thickened. Add cheese. Stir until melted.
Makes 1½ cups

Cherries Salad Dressing (Clemmons)

½ c vegetable oil
½ c vinegar (apple cider or white)
1 small Good Seasons Italian Salad Dressing
¾ c water
1 c Eagle Brand milk

Mix all ingredients well. Refrigerate.

Cole Slaw Dressing

1 (6oz) evaporated milk
⅓ c sugar
⅓ c vinegar
1 egg
1 t celery seed
1 t salt
dash pepper

Blend ingredients until smooth. Pour into saucepan cook and stir until thick. Chill.
Makes 1⅓ cups

Cooked Salad Dressing

¼ c sugar
1 t flour
1 t ground mustard
½ t salt
1 egg, lightly beaten
⅓ c white vinegar
2 T water
1 t butter
½ c mayonnaise

In a small saucepan, combine sugar, flour, mustard and salt. Stir in egg until smooth. Gradually add vinegar and water. Cook and stir over medium heat for 3 min, or until mixture reaches 160° and coats the back of a metal spoon. Remove from heat; stir in butter. Let stand 5 min. Stir in mayonnaise until smooth. Cover and refrigerate until chilled.

Yield: 1 - 1¼ cups

Cottage Dressing

Prepare 1 envelope garlic salad dressing mix according to directions. Shake well, then measure ½ cup of the dressing; to this amount add ½ cup large curd cream-style cottage cheese and 1 T catsup. Chill

Spoon over tomato or avocado slices.

Honey Fruit Dressing

1 c bottled oil vinegar dressing
¼ c honey
¼ c catsup

Combine ingredients in a jar or cruet; cover and shake well. Makes 1½ cups.

Creamy Fruit Dressing

Blend 1 T honey, 1 T lemon juice and 2 T orange juice into a 3 oz package of cream cheese. Add 1 t grated orange rind, ½ t salt and a dash of cayenne. Blend well. Slowly add ½ c salad oil, beaten until mixture is well mixed. Chill. Stir before serving.
Makes 1 cup

Fruit Salad Dressing

Mash 1¼ oz package of blue cheese and blend in ¼ c salad oil, 2 T lemon juice, ½ c cranberry juice, ½ t grated orange rind, 1 T orange juice, ⅛ t salt and ½ t sugar. Mix well.

Fruit Salad Dressing

⅔ c orange juice
3 T lemon juice
1 c sugar
1 egg, lightly beaten
Assorted fresh fruit

In a small saucepan, combine juices, sugar and egg. Bring to a boil; cook and stir for 1 min. or until thickened. Strain. Cover; refrigerate until serving. Serve with fresh fruit.

Yield: about 1 cup

Honey-Mustard Salad Dressing

3 T honey
2 T Dijon mustard
¼ c cider vinegar
½ c vegetable oil

In a small bowl, combine honey and mustard until smooth. Add vinegar; whisk until blended. Slowly add oil while beating with whisk.

Yield: 1 cup

Maraschino Cream Dressing

1 3 oz cream cheese, softened
2 T mayonnaise
1 T maraschino-cherry juice
1 T milk
1½ t lemon juice
1 T minced maraschino cherries

Combine first 5 ingredients; beat smooth. Stir in cherries. Chill. Makes about ⅔ cup

Marshmallow Dressing

To ½ jar marshmallow creme, add 1 T EACH orange juice and lemon juice; whip very fluffy with electric or rotary beater. Fold in ¼ c mayonnaise or salad dressing.
Makes about 1¼ cups

Mrs. Spiro Agnew's Spaghetti Sauce

1 lb ground beef (chuck or round)
½ t salt
½ t pepper
2 t Worcestershire sauce
1 small onion, chopped
½ green pepper, chopped
⅛ t garlic powder
¼ t oregano
1 (15 oz) tomato sauce

In skillet, lightly brown meat; add remaining ingredients and simmer for 30 min.

Pineapple Mustard Sauce

1 c brown sugar
1½ T cornstarch
2 T dry mustard
½ c water
½ c pineapple juice
½ c vinegar

Combine brown sugar, cornstarch and mustard in saucepan. Blend in ½ c water to make a smooth paste. Stir in pineapple juice and vinegar; cook over low heat, stirring, until thickened and clear.

Makes 2 cups

Poppy Seed Dressing – Lillian Johnson

1½ c sugar
2 t dry mustard
2 t salt
⅔ c vinegar
3 T onion juice
2 c salad oil (not olive oil)
2 T poppy seed

Mix sugar, mustard, salt and vinegar in blender. Add onion juice. Mix. Slowly add oil, beating constantly on low. Beat until thick and then beat 5 min. longer. Add poppy seeds.

Raisin-Nut Sauce for Baked Ham

Mix 1 T flour with ¼ c packed brown sugar. Add 1 c water. Bring to boiling point. Add ¼ t salt, 3 T lemon juice and ½ c seedless raisins. Simmer 5 min. Then add ¼ c chopped nuts and 1 T butter. Heat until butter melts.

Thousand Island Dressing #1

2 hard cooked eggs, chopped
dash salt
½ c drained pickle relish
1 c mayonnaise
¼ c chili sauce

In a bowl, mix mayonnaise, chili sauce, pickle relish and salt. Add chopped eggs. Chill dressing in the refrigerator.

Ashley and Rayvan

Thousand Island Dressing *

1 c mayonnaise
¼ c chili sauce
2 chopped hard-cooked eggs
2 T each
    chopped green pepper
    chopped celery
1 T finely chopped onion
1 t paprika
½ t salt

Mix well. Makes
2 cups.

237

Drinks

Anna Frances Dull's Hot Chocolate Mix

- ¾ c sugar
- ½ c creamer
- ½ c dry milk
- ⅓ c cocoa

Mix all together well. Store in closed glass jar. Use 2 heaping teaspoons per cup. Add hot water.

Citrus Mint Punch

1 c packed fresh mint leaves
Grated peel of 1 orange
Grated peel of 1 lemon
3 c boiling water
1 12oz frozen lemonade, thawed
1 12 oz frozen orange juice, thawed
1½ quarts cold water
Additional mint leaves, optional

Place mint and peels in a heat resistant pitcher or bowl; add boiling water. Let steep 1 hour; strain. Add concentrates and water; stir well. Chill. Serve over ice. Garnish with mint if desired.
Yield: 18–20 servings
(3 quarts)

Citrus Punch

1 12 oz frozen lemonade, thawed
1 12 oz orange juice, thawed
1 c sugar
1 t vanilla extract
1 t almond extract
8 c cold water
2 liters lemon-lime soda, chilled

In 2 large pitchers or a large punch bowl, combine the first 6 ingredients. Gently stir in soda. Serve immediately
Yield: 4 quarts

Cranberry-Pineapple Punch

1 48 oz cranberry juice drink
1 48 oz pineapple juice
½ c sugar
2 t almond extract

Stir together first 4 ingredients
until sugar dissolves. Cover
and chill 8 hours. Stir in
ginger ale just before serving.
Yield 26 cups

Sparkling Cranberry Punch

1 qt cranberry juice cocktail
1 6 oz frozen orange juice thawed and undiluted
1 6 oz frozen lemonade thawed and undiluted
2 c water
1 ¾ c ginger ale
orange slices (optional)

Combine first 4 ingredients; chill well.
Just before serving, pour mixture over
ice. Gently stir in ginger ale. Add
the orange slices if desired.
Yield: 2 ½ quarts

Doretha Black's Russian Tea

1 gal. tea
1 t cloves
2 t cinnamon
½ c lemon juice
1 qt orange juice
1 qt grape juice
1 lb. sugar

Dissolve sugar in hot tea. Add other ingredients and heat.
Yield: about 2 gallons

Easy Green Punch

2 small pkgs. Lemon-Lime Koolade
2 qts water
2 c sugar
1 48 oz pineapple juice

Mix all together. Be sure sugar is melted. When ready to serve add 1 qt. ginger ale.
Serves 30

Emerald Mint Punch

2 6 oz frozen pineapple juice undiluted
2 6 oz frozen lemonade undiluted
2 6 oz frozen limeade undiluted
Green food coloring
12 7 oz bottles lemon-lime carbonated beverage, chilled

Combine concentrates. Tint to desired shade with food coloring. Pour into 2 or 3 small molds and freeze. At serving time, dip one mold at a time into warm water. Put into punch bowl. Slowly pour on the beverage over concentrate; stir gently.
Makes about 30 4 oz servings

Good and Easy Punch
(Used for Murph's 90th birthday)

Equal parts
white grape juice
ginger ale

Serve cold —

Yellow Punch
(Used for Mom and Pappy's 50th anniversary)

1 large can orange juice
1 large can pineapple juice
1 or 2 small cans frozen lemonade (no water)
2 qts ginger ale or 1 2 lt. bottle

Mix all of first 3 ingredients
together. Add ginger ale last,

32 5 oz servings

Hint of Mint Lemonade

1¼ c water
½ c sugar
½ c fresh mint leaves, washed
½ package lemonade flavored drink mix
¼ c orange flavored breakfast drink

Boil water and sugar for 5 min.
Remove from heat and add fresh
mint leaves. Stir for a few
minutes and remove mint
leaves from syrup. Add
lemonade mix and stir to
dissolve. Add orange mix
and stir to dissolve. Chill
thoroughly. Serve over cracked
ice with a sprig of fresh
mint for garnish.

Hot Cranberry Punch

1 48 oz cranberry juice cocktail
1 c water
½ c packed brown sugar
¾ t ground cloves
½ t ground allspice
½ t ground cinnamon
¼ t ground nutmeg
1 48 oz pineapple juice

Combine first 7 ingredients in a large saucepan; mix well. Bring to a boil, stirring occasionally. Add pineapple juice; return to a boil. Reduce heat and simmer the punch 5 min. Serve hot.

Yield: 3 qts.

Instant Russian Tea

½ c instant tea
2 c Tang
1 pkg sweetened lemonade mix
½ – ¾ c sugar
½ t cinnamon
½ t allspice

Mix all ingredients well. Store in closed jar.
Use 3 t mix to 1 cup of hot water.

Minted Lemonade Syrup

2 c sugar
1 c water
½ c fresh mint leaves
1 c fresh lemon juice

Stir sugar and water in a small saucepan. Bring to a boil over medium heat. Crush mint leaves by twisting them or rubbing between palms of hands. Add to pan; boil 5 min. Remove from heat. Stir in lemon juice. Strain syrup into a glass container. Cover and store in refrigerator. For each serving stir 2 T syrup into 6 oz. of water. Makes 2½ cups, enough for 16 servings.

Mrs. Greenlaw's Hot Punch

Make in coffee pot
Put in bottom
  1 qt apple cider
  1 pt cranberry juice
  1 pt. orange juice
Put in top
  ½ c sugar
  1 t whole allspice
  3 sticks cinnamon

Let it go through the perk cycle.

Hot Spiced Percolator Punch

2 ½ c pineapple juice
1 ¾ c water
2 c cranberry juice
1 T whole cloves

½ t whole allspice
3 sticks cinnamon (broken)
1 t salt
½ c brown sugar

Put liquids in bottom part of an 8 cup electric percolator and the rest of the ingredients in the basket in the top. Perk for 10 min. or until the spices permeate. Serve hot,
  Makes 8 - 10 servings.

Mrs. Park's Russian Tea

3 lemons
2 oranges
1¼ c sugar
2 T tea
8 cloves
½ gal. boiling water

Put lemon and orange peel in bowl with cloves, tea and sugar. Pour boiling water over and let steep for 5 min. Strain. Then add fruit juices. You may add pineapple or other fruit juices as well.

Mrs. Park was Mildred Park's mother-in-law.

Peggy Leonard's Red Satin Punch

1 qt. apple juice
2 pts cranberry juice
10 7 oz bottles 7-Up
2 trays of 7-Up ice cubes

Mix first 3 ingredients.
Add ice cubes to punch bowl
to serve.

Yield: 35 servings

Salem College Iced Tea

4 sprigs fresh mint
8 - 12 whole cloves
3 qt water
1 ounce tea
Juice of 8 lemons
Juice of 6 oranges
1 48 oz can pineapple juice
1 lb. sugar

Add mint and cloves to water and
bring to a boil. Simmer for 10-15
min. Add tea and allow to steep
for 10 - 15 min.

Strain and, while still hot, add
fruit juices and sugar. That
step is important. Stir to
dissolve sugar.

Williamsburg Cider

1 gal. cider
½ c brown sugar
3 sticks cinnamon
1 t whole cloves
1 t whole allspice

Combine ingredients. Bring to a boil. Turn heat down and simmer for 20 min. Tie spices in cloth or strain mixture after simmering.

Egg Dishes

Amish Breakfast Casserole

1 lb sliced bacon, diced
1 med. sweet onion, chopped
6 eggs, lightly beaten
4 c frozen shredded hash browns, thawed
8 oz. shredded cheddar cheese
12 oz small curd cottage cheese
1¼ c shredded Swiss cheese

In a large skillet, cook bacon and onion until onion is crisp; drain. In a bowl, combine the remaining ingredients; stir in bacon mixture. Transfer to a greased 13 X 9 in baking dish.

Bake, uncovered, at 350° for 35-40 min. or until set and bubbly. Let stand 10 min. before cutting.

Yield: 12 servings

Bacon and Egg Casserole

1 (16 oz) Hawaiian bread cut in ¾ in cubes
   or 10-12 bread slices, cubed
2 c finely shredded Mexican 4 cheese blend
½ lb. (8 slices) bacon, cooked and crumbled
8 large eggs
2½ c milk
½ t pepper and ½ t salt
1 t dried mustard
½ t Worcestershire sauce
Salsa or sliced fresh tomatoes

Arrange bread cubes in lightly greased 9x13 in baking dish. Sprinkle with cheese and bacon. Whisk together eggs, milk, salt, pepper, mustard and Worcestershire sauce. Pour over prepared dish; press down bread cubes with a spoon to allow bread to soak up liquid. Cover and chill 8 hrs. Let stand 30 min. before baking. Bake 350° for 35 min or until set and golden. Serve with salsa or sliced tomatoes.
   Yield: 8-10 servings

Bacon Quiche

1 unbaked 9in pie shell

¼ c sliced green onions
1 T butter
6 eggs
1½ c heavy whipping cream
¼ c unsweetened apple juice
1 lb bacon, cooked and crumbled
⅛ t salt
⅛ t pepper
1 c (8oz) shredded Swiss cheese

In a small skillet, saute green onions in butter until tender. In a large bowl, whisk the eggs, cream and juice. Stir in the bacon, salt, pepper and green onions. Pour into pastry shell; sprinkle with cheese.

Bake at 350° for 40-45 min or until a knife inserted near center comes out clean. Let stand 10 min. before cutting.

Yield: 6 servings

Bacon Swiss Squares

2 c biscuit/baking mix
½ c cold water
8 oz sliced Swiss cheese
1 lb sliced bacon, cooked and crumbled
4 eggs, lightly beaten
¼ c milk
½ t onion powder

In a bowl, combine the biscuit mix and water; stir 20 strokes. Turn onto a floured surface; knead 10 times. Roll into a 14 x 10 in rectangle. Place on the bottom and ½ in. up the sides of a greased 9 x 13 x 2 in baking dish. Arrange cheese over dough. Sprinkle with bacon. In a bowl, whisk eggs, milk and onion powder; pour over bacon. Bake at 425° for 15 - 18 min. or until a knife inserted near the center comes out clean. Cut into squares; serve immediately.

Yield: 12 servings

Breakfast Casserole

2 slices bread
½ lb pork sausage
½ c shredded cheddar cheese
3 eggs
1 c milk
½ t ground mustard
¼ t salt
⅛ t pepper

Remove crust from bread and cut into 1 in. cubes. Place in greased 8 in. square baking dish. In a skillet, brown sausage over medium heat until no longer pink; drain. Sprinkle sausage and cheese over bread cubes.

In a bowl, whisk eggs, milk, mustard, salt and pepper. Pour over the sausage and cheese. Bake 350° for 30 min. or until puffed and golden.

2 - 4 servings

Graham Murphy

Broccoli Quiche

1 unbaked pie shell
1 box frozen broccoli
4 eggs
½ t salt
3 T Parmesan cheese
⅓ c grated cheddar cheese

Prebake pie shell at 400° for 10 min. Defrost broccoli in steamer for 15 min. Turn oven down to 350° Beat eggs slightly; add salt and 2 T Parmesan cheese. Add grated cheddar cheese. Stir to combine. Chop broccoli and add to egg mixture. Pour into pie shell and sprinkle with remaining Parmesan cheese. Bake for 20-25 min. Slice into 10 slices.

Cheddar Ham Oven Omelet

16 eggs
2 c milk
2 c (8 oz) shredded cheddar cheese
¾ c fully cooked ham, cubed
6 green onions, chopped

In a large bowl, beat eggs and milk. Stir in the cheese, ham and onions. Pour into a greased 13 x 9 in baking dish.
Bake, uncovered, at 350° for 40-45 min. or until a knife inserted near the center comes out clean. Let stand for 10 min. before cutting.

Yields: 12 servings

Egg Casserole

6 c cubed cooked ham
4 c (16oz) shredded cheddar cheese
8 c French bread cubes
3 T butter, melted
½ c all purpose flour
1 t dry mustard
8 large eggs
4 c milk

Layer ham, cheese and bread in a lightly greased 13 x 9 in. baking dish; drizzle with butter. Combine flour and mustard; sprinkle over top.

Whisk eggs and milk; pour over layers. Cover and chill for 8 hours.

Remove from refrigerator; let stand at room temperature 15 min.

Bake 350° for 50 - 55 min. or until set.

Yield: 8 - 10 servings

Ham 'n' Cheese Omelet Roll

4 oz cream cheese, softened
¾ c milk
2 T flour
¼ t salt
12 eggs
2 T Dijon mustard
2½ c cheddar or swiss cheese, divided
2 c finely chopped cooked ham
½ c thinly sliced green onions

Line bottom and sides of a greased 15×10 in baking pan with parchment paper; grease and set aside. In bowl beat cream cheese and milk until smooth. Add flour and salt. Mix until combined. In large bowl, beat eggs until blended Add cream cheese mixture; mix well. Pour into prepared pan.

Bake 375° for 30-35 min or until eggs are puffed and set. Remove and spread with mustard and sprinkle with 1c cheese.

Sprinkle with ham, onions and 1c cheese. Roll up from short side; peel off paper while rolling. Sprinkle top of roll with remaining cheese. Bake 3-4 min. longer or until cheese is melted. Slice. Makes 12 servings

Holiday Brunch Casserole

1 lb sausage
4½ c cubed day-old bread
2 c shredded sharp cheddar cheese
10 eggs, slightly beaten
4 c milk
1 t dry mustard
1 t salt
¼ t onion salt
Pepper to taste
½ c sliced mushrooms, optional
½ c peeled, chopped tomatoes, optional

Place bread in a well-buttered 9 X 13 in baking dish. Sprinkle with cheese. Combine the next 6 ingredients. Pour evenly over the bread and cheese. Sprinkle sausage and optional ingredients over the top. Cover and chill overnight. Preheat oven to 325°. Bake uncovered for about an hour. Tent with foil if top begins to brown too quickly.

Serves 6

Omelets in a Bag

Guests for breakfast? Here is an easy and fun way to prepare a tasty treat for breakfast (or anytime) Have guests use a permanent marker to write their names on a quart size self-locking freezer bag. Crack 2 large eggs into the bag (more than 2 will not work) Shake, mix well. Put out a variety of ingredients such as cheeses, ham, onion, green pepper, tomato, hash browns, salsa, etc. Have guests add the prepared ingredients of their choice to the bag and zip it up. Place the bags into rolling boiling water for exactly 13 min. You can usually cook 6-8 omlets in a large pot. For more, make another pot of boiling water. Open the bags and the omlet will roll out easily. Be prepared for everyone to be amazed. This is very nice to serve with fresh fruit and a coffee cake. It is a great conservation piece and everyone gets involved in the process.

Quiche Elaine

4 oz Muenster cheese
1 egg
¾ c flour
½ t salt
⅛ t pepper
1 c milk
¼ c chopped salami
½ t oregano

Chop cheese; save half for topping. Mix cheese with remaining ingredients. Pour into a well-greased 8 in. pie plate. Bake 20 min. at 425°. Sprinkle with remaining cheese and bake 10 min. longer.

Quiche Lorraine #1

1 pie crust 9 in.
Filling
12 strips bacon, cooked and crumbled
4 eggs
2 c half and half cream
1/4 t salt
1/8 t ground nutmeg
1 1/4 c shredded Swiss cheese

Sprinkle crumbled bacon in the chilled pie crust. In a bowl, beat eggs, cream, salt and nutmeg. Stir in cheese. Pour into crust. Bake at 425° for 15 min. Reduce heat to 325° and continue to bake for 30-40 min. or until a knife inserted near the center comes out clean. Let stand 10 min. before cutting.

Yield: 6 servings

Quiche Lorraine

2 pie shells
1 c diced ham or bacon
4 T butter
2 T chopped spring onions
1 can mushrooms
4 T white wine
3 eggs
1½ c milk

Bake shells until light and brown. Saute onions, mushrooms and ham in butter until tender. Add salt, pepper and wine, simmer 5 min. Beat eggs and milk together. Put cheese in pie shells. Mix all other ingredients and pour in pie shell. Bake at 375° for 30 min.

Serve with a small salad.

South of the Border Crustless Quiche

8 eggs, beaten
1 c flour
1 t baking powder
2 c cottage cheese
½ lb cheddar cheese, grated
½ lb Monterey Jack cheese, grated
¼ c butter, melted
7 oz can green chiles, sliced
1 c water chestnuts, sliced
½ small onion, chopped

Stir all ingredients together. Pour into a greased 2 quart flat baking dish. Bake at 375° for 30 - 40 min. or until set.

Yield: 6 - 8 servings

Meats

Apple-Stuffed Pork Chops

1½ c toasted ½ in bread cubes
½ c chopped apple
½ c shredded sharp cheddar cheese
2 T seedless golden raisins
¼ t salt
⅛ t ground cinnamon
2 T orange juice
2 T butter or margarine, melted
6 (1½ in) pork chops, cut with pockets
Salt and pepper to taste.

Combine first 4 ingredients; sprinkle with salt and cinnamon. Add orange juice and butter; stir until bread cubes are coated. Season pocket of pork chops with salt and pepper; stuff with bread cube mixture. Sprinkle chops with salt and pepper and place in shallow baking dish. Bake 350° for 1 hour and 15 min. Cover and bake an additional 15 minutes.
Yield: 6 servings

Linda Murphy and Frances Murphy

Slow Cooker

Autumn Pork Chops

4-6 boneless pork chops
2 c apple juice
½ t ground cinnamon

Place chops in slow
cooker. Cover with juice
Sprinkle with cinnamon
Cover and cook on low
for 10 hours.

4-6 servings

Menu idea
  Chops
  Potatoes
  Applesauce
  Cake

263

Baked Chicken in Wine Sauce
(Bud Lingenfelser)

10 split breasts, boneless and skinless
1 c cream of mushroom soup
1 c cream of chicken soup
1 c cream of cheddar cheese soup
½ soup can of white wine
Pepperidge Farm stuffing mix
(optional)

Spray baking pan with Pam. Mix and blend soups and wine until smooth. Lightly cover bottom of pan with soup mixture. Place chicken on bottom of pan; spread remainder of soup sauce over chicken. Spread stuffing mix lightly over sauce. Cover with foil and bake at 375° for ½ hour. Remove foil and bake about ½ hour or until done.

Note: Keep eye on stuffing so it won't burn.

Barbecue Hamburger

1½ to 2 lb hamburger
1 med. onion, chopped
Dash chili powder
1 can tomato soup
2 or 3 t mustard

Brown hamburger and onion together. Add chili powder, tomato soup and mustard. Simmer for 15 to 20 minutes. Serve on hamburger buns.

Slow Cooker

Barbeque

3 lb chuck roast
1 t garlic powder
1 t onion powder
salt and pepper to taste
1 18 oz bottle BBQ sauce

Place roast in slow cooker. Sprinkle with garlic and onion powder and season with salt and pepper. Pour sauce over meat. Cook on high 1 hour. Reduce heat to low and cook 5-7 hours more. Remove meat from cooker, shred and return to slow cooker. Cook 1 more hour. Serve hot.

8 servings

Beef Casserole

Grease casserole dish.
Spread 1 lb. ground beef
Sprinkle 1 t basil
Add layer of onions
                    potatoes
                    carrots
Pour on can of stewed tomatoe
Cover with bread crumbs
Bake 1 hr.   375° – 400°

Slow Cooker

Beef Stroganoff

1 lb stew beef
1 c golden mushroom soup
½ c chopped onion
1 T Worcestershire sauce
¼ c water
4 oz cream cheese

In slow cooker combin
all ingredients except cream
cheese. Cook on high 4–5
hours or on low 8 hours.
Stir in cream cheese just
before serving.

Serves 4

Beth Tartan's Best Meat Loaf

2 eggs
2 lb. good ground beef
1 envelope onion soup mix
1 8oz can tomato sauce
1 c uncooked rolled oats
1 T horseradish

Preheat oven to 325°. Beat eggs in a medium bowl and add remaining ingredients. Blend well — it takes hands to do a good job. Pack mixture into a greased loaf pan, Bake for about 1 hr. 15 min or until done. Remove from oven and allow to stand a few minutes before turning out.

Good!

Betty Carriker's Ham and Broccoli Bake

24 hours before serving
10 oz pkg. frozen chopped broccoli — partially cooked and drained
12 slices white bread. Cut each with doughnut cutter, Reserve rings but fit scraps into 13x9 in. pan
Layer: broccoli
    4 oz shredded cheddar cheese
    2 c cooked diced ham
Sprinkle with 2 t finely chopped onion
Arrange doughnuts on top
Combine 6 eggs, lightly beaten
    3½ c milk
    ½ t salt
    ¼ – ½ t dry mustard
Pour over bread. Cover and refrigerate 24 hours. Bake at 325° for 1 hour or until knife comes out clean. Let stand 10 min. before cutting

Betty Russell's Oven Fried Chicken

¼ c rice cereal crumbs
½ t pepper
½ t paprika
¼ t salt
4 (6 oz) skinned chicken breast halves
Butter-flavored cooking spray

Combine first 4 ingredients in a shallow bowl. Coat each breast with cooking spray; dredge in cereal mixture. Place on a baking sheet coated with cooking spray, and coat chicken again with cooking spray. Bake at 350° for about 50 min. or until done.

Yield: 4 servings

Good!

Broccoli Ham Roll-Ups

1 (10 oz) frozen chopped broccoli
1 (10¾ oz) cream of mushroom soup, undiluted
1 c dry bread crumbs
¼ c shredded cheddar cheese
1 T chopped onion
1½ t diced pimientoes
⅛ t dried rosemary, crushed
⅛ t dried thyme
Dash pepper
12 slices fully cooked ham (⅛ in thick)

Cook broccoli by package directions; drain. In a bowl, combine soup, bread crumbs, cheese, onion, pimientos and seasonings. Add broccoli; mix well. Spoon ¼ cups onto each ham slice. Roll up and place in an ungreased 9 X 13 X 2 in. baking dish. Cover and bake for 40 min. or until heated through.

Yield: 12 servings

Serve with cranberry relish, green vegtable and brownies.

Brunswick Stew for 4-6

¼ c butter
1 med. onion, chopped
1 green pepper, chopped
1 c celery, chopped
1 (16oz) can mixed okra, tomatoes and corn
1 (16 oz) can cream style corn
1 (6 oz) can tomato paste
2 c chopped cooked chicken,
   beef or pork (can use
   chicken and browned hamburger
1 T Worchestershire sauce
¼ t Tabasco
1½ t salt   (or less)
Black pepper to taste
1 c finely crushed bread crumbs (if needed

   Saute onion, pepper and celery in
butter. Mix with remaining ingredients
(except crumbs). Cover and cook
on low heat 45 min. stirring often.
If stew is not thick enough,
stir in bread crumbs just
before serving.

Slow Cooker

Can It Really Be So Easy?
Beef Roast

4 lt beef roast
1 (10¾ g) cream of mushroom soup
1 pkg. dry onion soup mix
1 c water

Place roast on double layer of foil. Combine soup and soup mix. Spread on all sides of roast. Wrap foil around roast and place in slow cooker. Pour water around the roast. Cover and cook on low 6-8 hours.

Serves 8

Chicken Biscuit Bake

1 can cream of chicken
    soup, undiluted
2/3 c mayonnaise
2-3 t Worcestershire
4 c cubed cooked chicken
3 c chopped broccoli, cooked
1 med onion, chopped

4 oz shredded cheddar cheese
2 (12 oz) tubes butter-
    milk biscuits
2 eggs
½ c sour cream
2 t celery seed
1 t salt

In bowl, combine soup, mayonnaise and Worcestershire. Stir in chicken, broccoli and onion. Pour in greased 9 x 13 baking dish. Sprinkle with cheese. Cover and bake at 375° for 20 min.

Separate biscuits; cut each in half. Arrange, cut side down, over the hot chicken mixture. In a small bowl, combine remaining ingredients. Pour over biscuits and bake, uncovered, 20 min. longer or until golden brown.

Serves 6-8 (or more)

Note: Reduced fat or fat free mayonnaise is not recommended for this recipe.

Chicken Cordon Bleu

$\frac{1}{3}$ c dry bread crumbs
$\frac{1}{2}$ t caraway seeds
4 4oz boneless, skinless chicken breast halves
2 oz thinly sliced deli ham
2 oz thinly sliced Swiss cheese
4 t Dijon mustard
Olive-oil flavored cooking spray

Preheat oven to 425°. Combine bread crumbs and caraway seeds in shallow bowl. Cut a horizontal slit through thickest part of each breast to form a pocket. Place ham and cheese evenly into pockets. Spread 1t mustard over each chicken breast, coating both sides. Dredge each breast in bread crumb mix, pressing firmly to coat. Coat lightly with cooking spray. Place chicken in 9 X 13 baking dish coated with cooking spray. Bake, uncovered, 22 - 25 min. or until chicken is done. Serve immediately.
    4 servings

Chicken Divan

2 pk. frozen broccoli
3 c chicken, cooked and sliced
2 c cream of celery soup, undiluted
1 c mayonnaise
1 t lemon juice
½ t curry powder
½ c sharp grated cheese
½ c bread crumbs
1 T butter

Cook broccoli until tender, drain and arrange in greased baking dish. Place chicken on top. Mix soup, mayonnaise, lemon juice and curry powder together and pour over chicken and broccoli. Top with grated cheese and refrigerate until ready to use. Top with bread crumbs and butter and bake at 350° for 30 min.

Chicken or Turkey Dressing

6 heaping cups bread crumbs
2 cups corn bread
3 eggs
½ cup milk
4 cups broth
1 t rubbed sage
2 t salt
½ t pepper

Mix thoroughly. Pour into a well-greased pan Bake at 400° until golden brown.

Chili

1 lb ground beef
½ c chopped onion
⅓ c chopped green pepper
1 clove garlic, minced
1 (16 oz) pinto or kidney beans, drained
1 (14½ oz) whole peeled tomatoes, chopped
1 (8 oz) tomato ~~paste~~ sauce
2 T A1 Steak Sauce
2 t chili powder
¼ t salt

In large skillet, cook and crumb meat until almost browned. Add onion, green pepper and garlic ~~tomato~~ Continue cooking until meat is browned and onion is tender. Stir in remaining ingredients Bring to boil; reduce heat. Cover and simmer 30 minut stirring occasionally.
Makes 4 servings

Chive-Ham Brunch Bake

½ c chopped onion
1 T butter
1 (5 oz) can chunk ham, drained
1 med. tomato, chopped
2 c biscuit/baking mix
½ c water
1 c shredded Swiss or cheddar cheese
2 eggs
¼ c milk
¼ t dill weed
¼ t salt and ⅛ t pepper
3 T minced chives

In a skillet, saute onion in butter until tender. Stir in ham and tomato. Set aside. Combine biscuit mix and water; mix well. Press onto bottom and ½ in. up the sides of a greased 9×13×2 baking dish. Spread ham mixture over crust; sprinkle with cheese. In a bowl, beat the eggs, milk, dill, salt and pepper; pour over cheese. Sprinkle with chives. Bake, uncovered, at 350° for 25-30 minutes or until a knife inserted near center comes out clean.

Yield: 8 servings

Country Style Steak
(Murphy's Restaurant)

3 lb. cubed beef
Salt and pepper
water
3 T flour

Heat oven to 400°. Place beef in Dutch oven or large saucepan. Season with salt and pepper. Cover with water. Place pot in oven and cook uncovered for about 2 hrs. until meat is tender. Pot should eventually just simmer; if it comes to a hard boil, reduce heat to 350° or lower as needed. About 30 min. before meat is finished, stir flour into 3 T water until smooth. Thoroughly stir flour mixture into meat then finish cooking in the oven. (The amount of flour mixture is approximate; it should thicken just slightly and be thinner than regular gravy.) Taste for salt and pepper and adjust if needed. Serve by itself or over cooked rice or mashed potatoes.

Slow Cooker

Crockpot Beef and Beans

1 large onion, chopped
1 green pepper, chopped
1½ lbs. hamburger
3 (1 lb) cans pork and beans
⅓ c brown sugar
1 c barbecue sauce
1 T mustard
1 T Worcestershire sauce
Dash Texas Pete

Brown onion, green pepper and hamburger in a frying pan. Put in crockpot and add rest of ingredients. Cover and cook 4 to 6 hours on low. Serve with slaw and crunchy bread.

Dinner in One Package

1½ lbs. steak (thick)
3 med. potatoes
1 pkg. onion soup mix
3 carrots
1 can cream of mushroom soup
Salt and pepper to taste

Place steak on foil. Sprinkle onion soup mix over steak. Quarter potatoes and cut carrots. Pour undiluted mushroom soup over steak then place the potatoes and carrots on foil around the steak. Sprinkle 1 t salt over vegetables and meat. Pepper to taste. Wrap and bake in 400° for 1½ hours or until done.

Easy Beefy Casserole

1 lb ground beef
¼ t salt
½ 16 oz frozen mixed vegetables
1 10½ oz cream of chicken soup
1 c shredded cheddar cheese
½ (32 oz) frozen seasoned potato tots

Preheat over 400°. Cook beef and salt over med. heat, stirring until meat crumbles and is no longer pink. Drain. Spoon into lightly greased 2½ qt. baking dish. Layer frozen vegetables, soup and cheese over beef. Top with frozen potatoes. Bake, uncovered, for 30 min. or until potatoes are golden.

Fancy Chicken Fingers

Marinate 1½ lb. chicken strips in mixture for 30 min.
¾ c buttermilk
½ t celery salt
½ t garlic powder
2-3 drops Tabasco
Then dip in 1½ c Italian seasoned bread crumbs and ¼ c parmesan cheese.
Place on cookie sheet and freeze. Bag and keep frozen until needed.
Bake at 450° for 12-15 minutes.
Spray pan and chicken with Pam so it will brown,

Frances Storey's Baked Chicken Breasts

Line baking dish with chipped beef. Debone 3 chicken breasts. Cut in half. Wrap breats tightly and then wrap with bacon. Secure with toothpicks. Lay on chipped beef.

Mix 1 can of cream of mushroom soup and 1 (8oz) carton of sour cream together. Pour over the chicken. Bake slowly at 300° for about 2 hours.

Serves 6

French's Chili

1 lb ground beef or turkey
1 red or green pepper, chopped
1 onion, chopped
1.25 oz pack chili seasoning mix
14.5 oz can whole tomatoes -
    undrained and cut up
15 oz can pinto beans, undrained
3 T Worcestershire sauce
1 T hot sauce (optional)

Brown meat, pepper and onion; drain. Stir in remaining ingredients. Bring to a boil then simmer, uncovered, for 10 min. Stir often. Serve with tortilla chips and shredded cheese if desired.

Makes 6 servings

Galax Easy Lunch or Dinner

1 thick hamburger patty
1 small potato, sliced
onion, sliced
carrot, sliced
Dry gravy mix
salt
pepper
1 small pat of butter
"Puddle" of catsup

On top of a sheet of aluminum foil place a thick hamburger patty on a "puddle" of catsup. Place the potato, onion and carrots on top of the hamburger. Add salt, pepper and butter. Sprinkle with the dry gravy mix. Wrap the aluminum foil around the meat and vegetables to make a package. Bake at 375° for about one hour. Makes 1 serving.

Note: Served with a fruit or green salad this makes and easy (and good) meal.

Hot Chicken Salad

2 c diced cooked chicken
1 c cream of chicken soup
½ c mayonnaise
3 hard cooked eggs, diced
½ c celery, diced
½ c sliced almonds
¼ c chopped onion

Combine all ingredients in a casserole dish. Bake at 350° 30-45 min. Sprinkle with cracker crumbs and extra almonds before serving.

Serving suggestion
Serve with fresh fruit salad, steamed asparagus and biscuits.

Ida's Chicken

Skin 8 chicken breasts
Add - Pepperidge farm dressing mix
Cream of chicken soup
Grated cheddar cheese
Drizzle on some butter
Cover with foil, Bake about an hour at 350°.

Ida's Chicken Salad

Cook 8 chicken breasts until tender. Chop
Add celery and pickle relish

Moisten with Miracle Whip and Hidden Valley LoCal dressing that you make up.

Impossible Bacon Pie

12 slices bacon, cooked and crumbled
⅓ c chopped onion
1 c shredded Swiss cheese
2 c milk
1 c Bisquick
4 eggs
¼ t salt
⅛ t pepper

Heat oven to 400°. Grease a 10 in pie pan. Sprinkle bacon, cheese and onion in bottom of pan. Beat remaining ingredients until smooth. (15 seconds on high) Pour into pie pan over mixture. Bake 35-40 minutes.

Jane Mendenhall's Chili for Hot Dogs

1 med. onion, chopped
1 lb. ground beef
¼ lb pork sausage
1 6oz can tomato paste
1 8oz can tomato paste
1 T Worcestershire sauce
Tabasco or other hot sauce to taste
1 t or more chili powder

Cook onion, beef and sausage together in a heavy skillet until lightly browned. Add remaining ingredients and simmer for about 15 min. The mixture is quite thick. For a thinner mixture, add a little water.

Margaret Brady's Meat Loaf

1 lb. ground beef
1 lb. ground sausage
1 large egg
1 med. onion, chopped
½ c milk
2 garlic cloves, grated
1 T chopped parsley
1 T curry powder
1 t salt
½ t pepper
1 c fine bread crumbs

Combine first 11 ingredients. Shape into 9 x 5 loaf pan. Bake 375° for 30 min. Pour half of sauce over meat loaf. Bake 45 more minutes. Serve with sauce.

Sauce for Margaret Brady's Meat Loaf

2 T butter
1 small onion, chopped
½ c Ketchup
¼ c brown sugar
¼ c water
¼ c beef broth
¼ c Worcestershire sauce
1 T instant coffee
2 T vinegar
2 t lemon juice

Melt butter in large skillet over med. heat. Add onion. Stir in ½ c Ketchup and remaining ingredients. Bring to boil, stirring constantly. Reduce heat. Simmer 10 min.

Marie Crisp's Chicken Pie

3 - 4 lbs. chicken breast
2 c chicken broth
1 can cream of chicken soup
1 stick margarine, melted
1 c self-rising flour
½ t black pepper
1 t salt
1 c buttermilk

Cook chicken until tender. Remove skin, take off bones and shred. Place in 9 X 13 in. dish. Bring to a boil 2 c chicken broth and cream of chicken soup. Pour over chicken. In a bowl, combine margarine, flour, pepper, salt and buttermilk. Pour or spoon over chicken. Bake at 425° for 30 - 4 min or until brown.

Serves 8 (or more)

Slow Cooker

No-Fuss Turkey Breast

5 lb turkey breast
1.35 oz dry onion soup mix
16 oz whole-berry cranberry sauce

Place turkey in slow cooker. Combine soup mix and cranberry sauce. Spread over turkey. Cover and cook on low 6 - 8 hours.

6 servings

Oven Beef Stew

2 lb beef cut into 1½ in cubes
2 med potatoes, peeled and cut in ½ in cubes
2 med onions, cut in ⅛ths
4 med carrots, cut in 1 in slices
3 celery ribs, cut in 1 in slices
1 11½ oz can tomato juice
⅓ c dry sherry or water
⅓ c quick cooking tapioca
1 T sugar
1 t salt
½ t dried basil
¼ t pepper
2 c fresh green beans, cut in 1 in slices

In Dutch oven, combine beef and vegetables, except beans. In a bowl, combine other ingredients. Let stand 15 min. Pour over beef mixture. Cover and bake 2 - 2½ hours or until meat is almost tender. Add the beans and cook about 30 min. longer or until beans and meat are tender.
8 servings

Grand Canyon, 1998

Oven Ham Croquettes

2 c ground cooked ham
½ c grated cheddar cheese
1 c soft fresh bread crumbs
1 t grated onion
1 egg, lightly beaten
salt to taste
¼ t pepper
¼ c melted butter or margarine
1 c fine cracker crumbs

Preheat oven to 375°. Grease a
10 x 6 x 1½ in baking dish.
In mixing bowl, combine
ham, cheese, bread crumbs, onion, egg,
salt and pepper. Mix well. Divide
mixture into 12 parts or more for
tiny croquettes; roll each to form
a cone. Roll in melted butter;
coat in cracker crumbs. Arrange
in pan.
Bake for 45 minutes or less
for smaller ones or until
golden. Turn once. Serve with
pineapple mustard sauce.

Peanut Pesto

1 c dry roasted peanuts
½ c soy sauce
¼ c honey
½ c water
1½ t minced garlic
½ c sesame oil
½ t pepper, or to taste

In a food processor, finely grind the peanuts. With motor running add the rest of the ingredients through the feed tube. Mix until the mixture becomes a smooth paste. Refrigerate until ready to use. This will keep for up to three days.

Makes 1½ c

Pecan-Crusted Chicken

Brush 4 medium skinless boneless chicken breasts on both sides with 2 T maple syrup.

On wax paper, combine ½ c finely chopped pecans, ½ c plain dried bread crumbs and ¼ t salt; use to coat chicken on both sides, pressing firmly so mixture adheres.

In a nonstick 12 inch skillet, melt 1 T butter with 2 T vegetable oil over medium heat.

Add chicken and cook until golden on the outside and no longer pink in the middle, 4 minutes per side.

Pet's Recipe for Cooking Country Ham

Soak ham all night or all day in plain water.
Put in a covered container
Add 4 or 5 c water.
Preheat oven 500° and put in ham. Let it come to a boil and cook for 20 min. Turn ham over and cook for another 20 min.
Turn oven off and leave ham in it until the oven gets cold.
Slice. thin.

Pot Roast

1   3-4 lb roast - chuck or eye round
1   12 oz can beer
1   (0.6g) Italian dressing mix

Brown roast on all sides in lightly oiled 5qt cast-iron Dutch oven over high heat. Remove from heat; add beer and dressing mix. Bake, covered, at 300° for 3 hours or until tender, turning once.

Yield: 6 servings

Slow Cooker

Pot Roast

2 cans cream of mushroom soup
1 pkg. dry onion soup mix
1¼ c water
1   5½ lb chuck roast

In slow cooker, mix soup, soup mix and water. Cut roast in half crosswise and place in cooker. Coat with soup mixture. Cook on high 3-4 hours or on low for 5-8 hours.

12 servings

Regal Chicken Salad

4 c diced cooked chicken
1 (13oz) pineapple chunks
1 c chopped celery
2 c seedless green grapes
⅔ c coarsely chopped salted peanuts
salt to taste
1 c mayonnaise
2 T lemon juice
2 T pineapple juice

Drain pineapple and reserve juice. Combine chicken, pineapple, celery, grapes, peanuts and salt. In another bowl, combine remaining ingredients. Fold two mixtures together; chill and serve on lettuce.

Serves 8 or more

Ritzy Chicken Casserole

1 chicken cooked and boned or
   3 lb. cooked breasts
3 c crumbled Ritz crackers
1 stick butter, melted
1 (10¼ oz) can cream of mushroom soup
½ c chicken broth
1 (8 oz) carton sour cream

Cook and bone chicken. Reserve broth. Cut chicken into bite-size pieces. Stir crumbled crackers into melted butter; place half the mixture in bottom of 9 x 13 in greased baking dish. Place chicken over crackers. Mix soup, chicken broth and sour cream; spoon over chicken. Top with remaining cracker crumb mixture. Bake in 375° oven for 40-45 min. or until bubbly and brown.

Robert Reed's Mother's Chicken Pie

Crust
2¼ c flour   ¾ c shortening
¼ c cold water   1 t salt
                    ⅛ t baking powder
Divide dough in halves for top and bottom crusts.

2 c chicken cut in 1 in pieces
1½ c rich broth
flour
Dash of pepper
1 T butter

Line 9 in pie dish with unbaked pastry.
Place in this the chicken and broth.
Sprinkle with flour, pepper and
dot with butter. Cover with
other half of dough and seal
edges thoroughly. Cut vent holes
in top crust. Bake until golden
brown in hot oven about 400°
to 425° for about 40-45 min.

This is what is called Moravian Chicken
Pie.

Ruthie Hyatt's Pork Chop Potato Bake

4 pork chops
2 c thinly sliced potatoes
1 med. onion, sliced
1 (10½ oz) cream of mushroom soup
½ c shredded cheese
salt

Butter casserole dish. Brown pork chops in hot oil. In casserole arrange layer of potatoes, onions, cheese and soup. Drain pork chops and lay on top of potatoes. Cover and bake 1 hour at 350°. Uncover and bake 15 min. longer to brown.

Sausage Biscuit Roll-Ups

2 lb sausage
4 c buttermilk baking mix
1 c milk
½ c margarine, melted

Combine baking mix, milk and butter. Knead. Refrigerate dough for 30 min. Divide dough in half. Roll out on lightly floured surface. Crumble half of the sausage over dough. Roll up like jelly roll. Repeat. Place in freezer for easier slicing. Cut in thin slices. Bake 400° for 10-15 min. or until done.

Southern Chicken Roll-Ups

6 boneless, skinless breast halves
6 slices Swiss cheese
3 T flour
½ t pepper
2 T butter or margarine
¾ c chicken broth
½ t dried oregano

Flatten chicken to ¼ in. thickness. Place a cheese slice on each; roll up jelly-roll style. In a shallow bowl, combine flour and pepper. Add chicken and roll to coat. In a skillet over med. heat, cook chicken in butter until browned, about 10 min., turning frequently. Add broth and oregano; bring to a boil. Reduce heat; simmer for 12-14 min. or until chicken juices run clear.

Yield: 6 servings

Spread for Ham Sandwiches

3 T mustard
3 t Poppy seed
1 stick margarine – softened
1 t Worcestershire sauce
Small onion chopped fine

Mix all together well.

Stew Beef Casserole

1 bell pepper
2 potatoes
2 onions
3 carrots
2 stalks celery
1 lb beef
1 t salt
½ t pepper
4 T Worcestershire sauce
½ c water

Cut vegetables and mea
as for stew. Put in a
foil lined pan. Add
seasonings and water.
Wrap airtight. Cook
2 hours at 350°.

Sweet and Sour Meatballs

1 20oz pineapple chunks
½ c brown sugar
3 T cornstarch
⅓ c cold water
3 T cider vinegar
1 T soy sauce
30 frozen fully cooked meatballs, thawed
1 large green pepper cut into 1 in. pieces

Drain pineapple; reserve juice. Add water to juice to measure 1 cup. Pour into large skillet. In a bowl, combine brown sugar, cornstarch, cold water, vinegar and soy sauce until smooth. Stir into skillet. Bring to boil over med. heat; cook and stir until thickened. Add pineapple, meatballs and green pepper. Simmer, uncovered, for 20 min. or until heated through.

Serves 6

Swiss Steak

3 T olive oil
½ c flour
½ t salt
pepper to taste
3 lb. round steak
2 onions, coarsely chopped
2 c canned tomatoes

Mix flour, salt and pepper. Pound seasoned flour into both sides of steak. Brown meat well on both sides in a large skillet. Top with onions and tomatoes. Cover tightly and simmer 1 - 1½ hours, depending on thickness and tenderness of the meat cut. This makes its own sauce!

Slow Cooker

There's No-Easier Roast Beef

12 oz bottle barbeque sauce
3-4 lb. beef roast

Pour ½ of BBQ sauce into bottom of cooker. Add meat. Top with remaining sauce. Cover. Cook on low 6-8 hours. Slice and serve with sauce

Serves 6-8

Slow Cooker

Turkey Breast

6 lb turkey breast
2 t oil
salt and pepper to taste
1 med onion, quartered
2-4 garlic cloves, peeled
½ c water

Rinse turkey and pat dry with paper towels. Rub oil over turkey. Sprinkle with salt and pepper. Place, meat side up, in cooker. Place onion and garlic around sides. Cover. Cook on low 9-10 hours or until meat thermometer stuck in meaty part reads 170°. Remove from cooker, Let stand 10 min. before slicing.

Serve with mashed potatoes, cranberry salad and beans.

Serves 8-10

Slow Cooker

What If Ham

3-4 lb fully cooked ham
12 oz lemon-lime soda
¼ c honey
½ t dry mustard
½ t ground cloves
¼ t cinnamon

Place ham in slow cooker. Add soda. Cover and cook on low 6-8 hours or high for 3-4 hours. About 30 min before serving, combine 3 T juice from cooker with honey. Mix well and spread over ham. Cover and continue cooking on low for 30 min. Let stand 15 min. before slicing.

12 - 16 servings

Yummy Chicken Balls

3 5oz cans white chicken
½ t Worcestershire sauce
½ t lemon juice
1 t dried parsley
1 t dried chives
½ t minced garlic
1 egg
¼ c bread crumbs
Vegetable oil for cooking

Rinse and drain chicken. Flake meat until very fine. Add all ingredients except egg, bread crumbs and oil. Add egg, then bread crumbs. Blend well, form into quarter size balls and refrigerate at least an hour. Add oil to frying pan to a depth of about ¼ in. Heat the oil then add a few balls at a time and cook until golden brown on both sides.
Serve hot with Peanut Pesto

Pickles and Relished

Beth Tartan's Strawberry Preserves

1 qt. strawberries
4 c sugar
2 T fresh lemon juice

Bring strawberries and 2 cups of sugar to a boil. Boil 5 min. Add other 2 cups sugar and lemon juice. Let boil 10-15 min. more. Pour into a dish (earthenware if you have one). Cover. Let stand for 24 hours. Put into sterilized jars. Cover with paraffin.

Bread and Butter Pickles

Mix together
4 quarts sliced cucumbers
6 sliced onions
1 red sweet pepper
⅓ c salt

Put 2 trays of ice cubes on top of the above mixture and let set for 3 hours. Drain and rinse. Then mix with
3 c cider vinegar
3½-4 c sugar
1½ t celery seed
2 T mustard seed
1½ t tumeric

Bring to a boil and pack in sterilized jars. (Do not overcook.)

Makes 3½ quarts

Delicious Pepper Relish

12 green peppers
12 red peppers
12 med. onions
1 hot pepper

Grind the above. Pour on boiling water and let stand 10 min. Drain and bring to a boil in:

½ c sugar
2 T salt
2 c vinegar

Bring to boil then simmer gently for about 10 min. Seal in sterilized jars.

Disappearing Pickles

12 cucumbers (5 in)
4 onions, sliced
4 c sugar
4 c cider vinegar
½ c salt
1¼ t tumeric
1¼ t celery seed
1¼ t mustard seed

Wash cucumbers and cut into ¼ in slices. Layer cucumbers and onion slices in a gallon jar. Combine sugar and remaining ingredients; stir well. Pour vinegar mixture over layered cucumbers and onions. Cover and chill at least 24 hours.

Makes 1 gallon

Ginny Burton's   Chow Chow

4 c onions	6 c sugar
1 med. cabbage	1 T celery seed
10 green tomatoes	2 T mustard seed
12 green peppers	1½ t tumeric
6 red peppers	4 c vinegar
½ c salt	2 c water

Chop vegetables fine. Sprinkle with salt. Let stand covered with foil, overnight. Next morning rinse and drain.

Combine remaining ingredients and pour over vegetables. Heat to boiling. Simmer 3 minutes. Pack into sterilized jars and seal. Process 10 min in hot water bath. Tighten lids again when you take them out of the water.

Makes about 10 pints

Ginny Burton's Cucumber Pickles

1 gallon jug

14 c sliced, not peeled, cucumbers
2-4 c sliced onion
4 T salt
2 T celery seed
2 c sugar
2 c vinegar
2 green peppers, sliced

Mix all together. Let stand 30 minutes. Pour into gallon jug.

These need to be kept in the refrigerator. They will last for a long time.

Hot Pepper Jelly

3/4 c ground bell pepper
1/4 - 1/2 c ground hot pepper
1 1/2 c cider vinegar
6 1/2 c sugar
Green food coloring
1 (6 oz) bottle Certo

Combine all ingredients, except Certo, in a saucepan and bring to a boil. Continue boiling for 5 min. Take off heat and add Certo. Stir well. Pour into sterilized jars and seal. (note: wear gloves when handling hot peppers.)

* Another similar recipe adds 1/2 t salt and 10 drops food coloring.

Makes about 4-5 1/2 pt. jars

Ice Box Pickles

1½ c vinegar
1 c sugar
1½ T celery seed
1 t salt
8 sliced med. cucumbers

Boil salt and sugar with vinegar and seed until dissolved. Allow to cool then pour over sliced cucumbers. Keeps in the refrigerator for 3-4 weeks.

(I needed a little more syrup to cover the cucumbers.)

Jane Reed's Bread and Butter Pickles

1 gal cukes
3 c vinegar
4 c sugar
4 t celery seed
4 t tumeric
4 T salt
4 t mustard seed

Place all ingredients in a large container. Let come to a boil. Stir until all cukes are covered with mixture. Do <u>not cook</u>! Place in jars and seal.

Honoring Veterans

Lazy Housewife Pickles

Scrub cukes. Thinly slice into jars. Add slice of raw onion or a few onion flakes and ½ t celery seed to each jar.

Boil and pour into each jar this syrup.

1 c cider vinegar
1 c sugar
1 t salt

Seal in sterilized jars. Ready after a few days.

Mom Kite's Chow Chow

1 gallon cabbage
1 gallon green tomatoes
1/4 pt. hot red and green peppers
1 qt. onions
1/2 gallon green and red bell peppers
1 c salt
2 qts. vinegar
4 T dry mustard
2 T ground ginger
1 T celery seed
2 lbs. sugar

Remove seeds from peppers and chop all vegetable very fine. Add salt and let stand overnight in an earthen jar. Next morning, squeeze out all liquid. Add other ingredients; cook without a lid until tender. (Probably a little longer than an hour.) Put a wire trivet between pot and heat element. Cook to a rolling boil and then reduce heat to medium. When tender seal in glass jars.

Mom Krites Pickled Peaches

1½ c vinegar
1 c water
4-5 c sugar

Tie in a bag
  3 sticks cinnamon (break
    into small pieces)
  1 T whole cloves

Cook about 5 minutes and
then put in peaches. Cook
until they are tender. Put
in hot, sterilized jars and
seal.

(If you cook 2 cookings,
put in another cup of
sugar.)

Mom Krites Strawberry Preserves

3 quarts (before capped) berries
6 cups sugar

Cook on high heat. When
they boil really well, cook
10 min. Stir to keep from
sticking. Pour out in
shallow pans and let
stay in the sun until
they are thick enough:

Mrs. Brann's Chow-Chow Relish

2-3 onions chopped
cabbage — big head - chopped
green tomatoes — 12 or more, chop
red and green peppers 8-10 chop
Hot pepper — according to how
    hot you like it   chop
celery — several stalks (almost all)
                       chop

Chop up vegetables and
sprinkle with salt.
Bring to a boil
    4 c sugar
    1½ t celery seed
    1½ t mustard seed
    3 c vinegar
    1½ t tumeric

Squeeze out vegetables and
put in vinegar mix. Let it
cook up well — about 10 min.
Put in sterilized jars and
seal.

Murph's Mom's Peach Preserves

1¼ lb. peaches
1 lb. sugar
Add a little water to begin
the cooking process.

Cook until tender and
thickened. Put into sterile
jars and seal with wax

Orange Peach Marmalade

12 peaches
3 oranges
1½ T lemon juice
Sugar

Peel, pit and chop peaches;
sliver half the peel of the oranges;
cover with water and boil until
the peel is tender. Drain.
Add the cooked orange peel, orange
pulp and lemon juice to the peaches
and measure. Add ¾ c sugar for
each cup of fruit and boil
rapidly for 25-30 min. or
until thick, stirring frequently
to prevent burning. Pour
hot into hot sterilized jars
and seal.

Refrigerator Pickles

8 c thinly sliced cucumbers
1 c thinly sliced onion
1 c green pepper
2 T salt

Sprinkle salt over vegetables and let stand 1 hour, stirring several times.

1 c vinegar
1½ c sugar
1 T celery seed
1 T mustard seed

Boil ingredients together. Drain vegetables about 10 min. but do not rinse. Pack cucumbers in container and pour liquid all over. Do not use for 24 hours. Will keep in refrigerator up to a year.

Stuffed Peppers #1

Shred cabbage and add some salt. Cut the ends out of the peppers, remove seeds and stuff with cabbage. Place in jars.
Make a solution of
1 c vinegar (Mom K says about ¾ c)
1 c water (Mom K says 1¼ c)
½ c sugar or to taste
Bring to a full boil.

Pour over peppers and tighten lids. Process in hot water bath for 10 min. (Time from when water starts to boil)

Tighten lids again when you take jars from hot water.

Stuffed Peppers #2

small green peppers	vinegar
cabbage	water
salt	vinegar
	sugar

Cut a hole in stem end of peppers and remove seeds. Shred cabbage and sprinkle with salt to taste. Mash cabbage with hands to bruise it. Pack cabbage in peppers. Turn peppers over and press open end with fingers to remove excess water. Prepare liquid. In a saucepan put 1 cup water, 1 c vinegar and ½ c sugar. Bring to a boil.

Pack peppers in hot, steril. jars. Pour the hot liquid into the jars leaving ¼ in headspace. Press down on peppers on top to remove any air bubbles. Add 2 piece lids.

Process 15 min. in a water-bath canner. Tighten rings again when removed from canner.

Sweet Dill Pickles

1 qt. whole Kosher dill pickles
1 c sugar
1 t mustard seed
½ t crushed garlic

Drain and wash pickles 3 times in cool running water. Slice pickles into a bowl and add sugar, mustard seed, and garlic. Leave at room temperature 12-14 hours, then refrigerate, covered. These keep a long time.

Sweet Pickles

Day 1 - Wash 1 gal. cukes and place in crock. Bring to boil 1 gal water and 2 c canning salt. Pour over cukes. Be sure all are covered. Cover with cloth. Let stand 24 hrs.

Day 2 - Drain salt water off. Bring to boil 1 gal water and 1 container of alum. Pour over cukes and let stand 24 hours.

Day 3 - Drain alum water. Boil 1 gal. plain water and pour over cukes. Let stand 24 hours

Day 4 - Drain water. Boil 1 gal white vinegar Pour bottle of pickling spices over cukes. Pour vinegar over cukes. Let stand 24 hours.

Day 5 - Slice cukes in large pan. Layer cukes and sugar in a large jar. (Sugar layer should be heavy.) When sugar has melted be sure you have enough syrup to cover cukes well. When all is melted you keep in refrigerator forever. You can put in small jars before refrigerating.

* If you lack enough liquid to cover add a little more water and vinegar.

Good !!!

Pies

Alice Johnson's Ice Cream Pie

1 c canned milk
1 c small marshmallows
1 c chocolate semi-sweet morsels
1/4 t salt

Melt over medium heat until completely melted and thickened. Remove and cool to room temperature.

1 quart ice cream

Put half of ice cream over crust. Cover with half of chocolate mixture. Put rest of ice cream and then rest of chocolate.

Decorate with pecans on top and freeze until firm 3-5 hours.

This may be put in a baked or other kind of crust.

(Alice Johnson's) Walnut Sauce

1 c light corn syrup
1/8 t salt
1/4 c water
1/4 t maple flavoring
1 c walnuts or pecans

In heavy saucepan, mix corn syrup, salt, water and maple flavoring. Add coarsely chopped nuts. Bring to a boil, cover and simmer for about 25 min. Cool and cover tightly. Refrigerate. Makes about 2 cups.

Angel Pie

Meringue shell

4 egg whites
¼ t cream of tartar
1 c sugar

Beat egg whites until light, not dry. Add cream of tartar. Mix well. Add sugar gradually; beat until peaks form. Place in well-greased pie plate not too near edge. Bake 250° for 40 min.

Filling

4 egg yolks
½ c sugar

4 T lemon juice
1 c whipped heavy cream
or Cool Whip

Beat egg yolks until light yellow. Add sugar and lemon juice. Cook in double boiler over low heat until thickened. Whip cream but do not sweeten. (I used Cool Whip) Place ½ whipped cream or Cool whip in shell. Spread cooled lemon filling over cream; top with remaining whipped cream or Cool Whip. Place in refrigerator at least 24 hours before serving.

Serves 6 - 8

Beth Tartan's Foolproof Pie Crusts

4 c flour, lightly spooned into cup
1 T sugar
2 t salt
1 ¾ c vegetable shortening
1 large egg
½ c cold water
1 T vinegar

1. Whisk together flour, sugar and salt in large bowl. Cut in shortening with a pastry blender until crumbly.
2. Beat egg, water and vinegar in a bowl. Add to flour mix and stir until ingredients are moistened.
3. Divide dough into 5 portions. Shape into a flat round patty ready for rolling. Wrap in plastic or waxed paper and chill at least ½ hour.
4. To make shell, lightly flour both sides of patty and roll it out on a floured board. Ease into 9 in pie plate. Fill and bake 350° for 40-45 min.

Makes 5 single crusts   20 tart shells

Brenda Smith's Cobbler

Melt 1 stick of butter in a 9X13 in pan.

Mix together
1 c self-rising flour
½ c sugar
1 c milk
pinch of salt
Add to butter in the pan

Mix 3 c peaches with
¾ c sugar
Add to pan.

Bake 350° for 45 min. or until golden brown.

Brown Sugar Pie

1 unbaked 9 in pie shell
3 c brown sugar
¾ c melted butter
¾ c milk
3 eggs
3 T flour
1 t vanilla
½ t salt

Beat all ingredients together in large bowl of electric mixer. Pour into crust. Bake at 350° for 45 min. or until set. If desired, top with whipped cream.

(Jane Mendenhall) Chocolate Angel Pie

2 egg whites
1/8 t salt
1/8 t cream of tartar
1/2 c sifted sugar
1/2 c chopped nuts

1/2 t vanilla
1 Baker's German Sweet Chocolate
3 T water
1 t vanilla
1 c whipping cream

Beat egg whites until soft peaks form. Add sugar gradually, and beat until mixture is very stiff. Fold in nuts and vanilla. Turn into lightly greased 8 in pie pan and make a nest-like shell, building sides up 1/2 in above edge of pan. Bake in slow oven (300°) 50 -55 min. Cool.

Place chocolate and water in saucepan over low heat. Stir until chocolate is melted. Cool until thickened. Then add 1 t vanilla.

Whip cream. Fold chocolate mixture into whipped cream. Spoon into the meringue shell. Chill about 2 hours before serving.

If you like a sweeter chocolate, add 1/2 c sugar to cream when whipping.

Chocolate Chess Pie

1 c light brown sugar
4 eggs
1½ c sugar
4 T flour
4 T cocoa
½ t salt
1 t vanilla
1½ c canned milk
4 T melted butter

Add eggs to sugars and beat together. Add other ingredients. Pour into unbaked pie shells. Bake at 325° for 45 min. to an hour or until set. Makes 2 deep dish pies or can be made into tarts.

To make Lemon Chess substitute lemon rind, lemon extract and lemon juice for cocoa.

Chocolate Chess Pie
(Robert Reed's mother)

2 eggs, beaten
1½ c sugar
¼ c cocoa
1 t flour
½ stick margarine, melted
1 t vanilla
½ c canned milk

Beat all together. Place in unbaked pie shell. Bake 325° for 35 min or until set.

Chocolate Fudge Pies

2½ c sugar
1½ t flour
1 t cornstarch
2 eggs, beaten
1 T vanilla
½ stick butter, melted
1 (12oz) can evaporated milk
½ c cocoa
2 unbaked pie shells

Combine first three ingred and mix well. Add eggs and vanilla. Mix well. Add other ingredients and mix well. Pour evenly into pie shell. Bake 350° for 30 min to 45 min. or until set. Let stand to cool. Serve w/ whipped cream.

12 servings

Chocolate Pecan Pie

2 squares chocolate
2 T butter
3 eggs, beaten
½ c sugar
¾ c dark corn syrup
¾ c pecan halves
1 9in unbaked pie shell

Melt chocolate and butter together. Add beaten eggs, sugar and syrup. Mix in pecan halves. Pour into pie shell. Bake at 375° for 40-50 min until set. Serve warm or cold with whipped cream or ice cream.

Chocolate Ribbon Pie

4 oz cream cheese, softened
2 T sugar
1 T milk
1 8 oz Cool Whip, divided
1 prepared chocolate crust
2 c cold milk
2 (4 serve) chocolate instant pudding
and pie mix

Beat cream cheese, sugar and 1 T milk in large bowl until smooth. Gently stir in ½ of Cool Whip. Spread on bottom of crust.

Pour 2 c milk into large bowl. Add pudding mixes. Beat with a wire whisk 2 min. Pour over cream cheese layer.

Refrigerate 4 hours or until set. Just before serving, spread remaining Cool Whip over pudding layer. Garnish with shaved chocolate or chocolate curls.

8 servings

Coconut Pie Crust

2 c flaked coconut
2 T sugar
1 T flour
2 T margarine, melted

Combine coconut, sugar and flour. Blend in margarine. Press mixture into 9 inch pie plate. Bake 350° for 10 min. Chill.

Good Filling Tropical Parfait Pie
1 3oz lime Jello
1 c boiling water
1 pt vanilla ice cream
2 c miniature marshmallows

Dissolve Jello in water. Add ice cream. Stir until melted. Chill until almost firm. Fold in marshmallows. Pour into coconut crust. Chill until firm.

Coconut Tarts/Pie

3 beaten eggs
1½ c sugar
½ c butter, melted
4 t lemon juice
1 t vanilla
1 (3½oz) can (1⅓ c) flaked coconut

Combine eggs, sugar, butter, lemon juice and vanilla. Stir in coconut. Pour into unbaked tart shells or pie shell. Bake in 350° oven 40 min or until knife comes out clean. Cool before serving.

Makes 8 tarts
          1 9 in pie

Double Layer Chocolate Pie

4 oz cream cheese, softened
1 T milk
1 T sugar
1 8oz Cool Whip
1 chocolate crumb crust
2 c cold milk
2 (4 serve) chocolate instant pudding

Mix cream cheese, 1 T milk and sugar in bowl with wire whisk until smooth. Gently stir in 1½ c Cool Whip. Spread on bottom of crust.

Pour 2 cups cold milk into bowl. Add pudding mix. Beat with wire whisk until well mixed. Immediately stir in remaining Cool Whip. Spread over cream cheese layer.

Refrigerate 4 hours or until set. Garnish with additional Cool Whip if desired. Store leftover pie in refrigerator.

8 servings

Dream Pie

1 can condensed milk
1 can red pie cherries, pitted and drained
1 can fruit cocktail, drained
½ c lemon juice
1 envelope whipped topping mix
1 c chopped nuts
2 prepared pie shells

Blend milk, cherries, fruit cocktail and lemon juice. Prepare topping mix by package directions and fold in with nuts. Pour into pie shells. Chill until firm.

(I use Cool Whip instead of topping mix.)

Easy Apple Pie

¾ c sugar
¼ c flour
½ t cinnamon
Dash salt
6 c thinly sliced apples, peeled
1 unbaked pie shell
3-4 pats butter

Preheat oven to 350°.
In a bowl, mix sugar, flour, cinnamon and salt. Toss in apples to coat. Pour into pie shell. Dot the top with pieces of butter. Bake until apples are soft, about 1 hour.
Makes 1 pie

Egg Custard Pie

2 eggs
¼ c + 2 T sugar
1 t vanilla
1½ c scalded milk
1 unbaked pie shell
nutmeg

Beat eggs, sugar and vanilla. Add scalded milk. Pour into pie shell. Sprinkle nutmeg over top. Bake at 450° for 20 min. or until done.

Exquisite Pie

2 eggs
1 c sugar
½ c coconut
½ c chopped nuts
½ c raisins
½ stick margarine, melted
1 T vinegar

Mix all ingredients and pour in unbaked 9 in. pie shell. Bake 325° for about 40 min.

5 Minute Pudding Pie

1¼ c cold milk
2   4 serve instant pudding - any flavor
1   8 oz Cool Whip - divided
1 Graham cracker or baked crust

Beat milk, pudding mix and ½ of Cool Whip in bowl with a wire whisk for 1 min. Mixture will be thick Spread in crust.

Spread remaining Cool Whip over pudding layer – Serve immediately or refrigerate until ready to serve.

Makes 8 small servings
6 medium servings

Fluffy Lime Pie

1 envelope (13 oz) lime soft drink mix
1 can condensed milk
1 8 oz Cool Whip
1 graham cracker crust

In large bowl, dissolve soft drink mix in milk; fold in Cool Whip. Spoon into crust. Cover and refrigerate for 3 hours or until set.

Yield: 6-8 servings

Fool Proof Pie Crust

1½ c sifted flour
1 t baking powder
5 T shortening
½ t salt
4 T cold water

Mix flour with baking powder and salt. Blend in shortening and add water to make a soft dough. Roll and shape into pie pan. Makes a 9in pie with top.

Impossible Coconut Pie

½ c self-rising flour
4 eggs, well beaten
½ stick melted butter
2 t vanilla
2 c milk
7 oz flaked coconut (about 2½ c)

Heat oven to 350°. Lightly grease 2 pie pans or spray them with cooking spray.

Mix sugar and flour together; add eggs, melted butter, milk and coconut. Mix well.

Bake 35-40 min. or until brown on top. Let cool before slicing.

Makes 2 pies

(Jane Mendenhall) Ice Cream Pie

2 1 oz squares unsweetened chocolate
2 T butter
2 T milk
⅔ c sifted confectioner's sugar
1½ c shredded coconut
   (1 can for pie)
1½ qt vanilla ice cream, soften
2 t instant coffee (optional)
½ c nuts

Melt chocolate and butter. Stir milk into sugar. Add to chocolate mix. Mix well and stir in coconut. Spray pie pan with non-stick spray and press mix into it to make crust. Put in the refrigerator to cool. Mix ice cream, coffee and nuts. Fill crust. Freeze.

(I don't use coffee.)

Jane Reed's Fruit Cobbler

Use cherries, peaches or blueberries

4 slices bread - cubed and put in
   bottom of pan.
Add fruit of choice
Mix together and pour over fruit
   1 stick melted butter
   1 egg
   ¾ c sugar
   1 T flour

Bake in 350° for 40 min.

(Jean Whitley) Japanese Fruit Pie

   2 eggs - beaten
   ¾ stick margarine - melted
   1 c sugar
   ½ c flaked coconut
   ½ c raisins
   ½ to 1 c chopped pecans
   1 t vinegar
   dash salt

   1 unbaked pie shell

   Beat eggs and add remaining
ingredients. Pour into pie
shell. Bake in 350° preheated
oven about 45 min.

   Can be made into tarts
as well.

(Murph's Favorite)   Key Lime Pie

1 can condensed milk
4 eggs, separated
½ c key lime juice
one 8 or 9 in pie shell (baked)
½ c sugar

Preheat oven to 450° to brown meringue.

Pour milk into mixer bowl. Add egg yolks and beat at moderate speed for 2 minutes.

Stop mixer. Slowly pour lime juice into milk-egg mixture. With spoon gently fold juice into mixture. Do not beat. Pour into pie shell.

Beat egg whites to hold a peak then gradually add sugar.

Pile meringue around outer edge then work inward. Use all of the meringue.

Brown until golden — about 5 min.

Lemon Chess Pie

2 c sugar
1 T flour
1 T corn meal
4 eggs
½ stick butter, melted
¼ c milk
¼ c grated lemon zest
¼ c lemon juice
1 unbaked 9 in pie shell

Combine sugar, flour and cornmeal. Mix well. Beat in other ingredients until smooth. Pour into pie shell. Bake 350° for 40 min or until top is brown.

6 servings

Mama's Sugar Pie

1 egg
1 c brown sugar
1 t vanilla
½ c butter
2 T water

Cream butter and sugar. Add well-beaten egg, water and vanilla and set aside. Make crust and bake in slow (325°) oven until set.

Mildred Park's Pecan Pie

3 eggs – beat slightly
Add 1 c Karo syrup
½ c sugar
1 t salt
1 c chopped pecans
1 t vanilla

Pour into unbaked pie shell. Bake 350 for 50 min.

(Mildred Tester) Pineapple Pie

Melt 1 stick margarine
Add 1 c sugar
Beat in 4 eggs, one at a time
Add 1 c coconut
    1 small can crushed
      pineapple and juice
    1 t vanilla

Pour into 2 unbaked
pie shells. Bake 350°
for about 40 min.

Millionaire's Pie

2 9 in. Graham cracker crusts
1 (#2½) can peach slices
1 can crushed pineapple
½ c lemon juice
1 8 oz Cool Whip
1 can condensed milk
chopped pecans

Drain peaches and chop;
combine with drained pineapple
and remaining ingredients.
Turn into crumb crusts and
sprinkle with pecans.
Chill.
    Makes 2 pies

Mom Krites' Pumpkin Pie

1 big or 2 little eggs
1 big cup pumpkin
¾ c sugar
pinch salt
little can canned milk
 (big can makes 2 pies)
T (scant) flour
1 t or more pumpkin pie spice

Mix all together and put
in unbaked pie shell.
Bake 400° for a little
bit and then cut down
to 350° until done.

Mom Krites' Strawberry Pie

½ c sugar
2 T flour
salt
1 eggs

Beat all up together. Add
1 c milk or a little more.
Have a raw crust. Sprinkle
flour in bottom. Put in
strawberries (about a pint).
Sprinkle with flour. Sprinkle
heavier with sugar (about
a scant cup). Pour cream
stuff on it. Bake 350°
about 30 min. or until
custard gets stiff.

(I wrote this down as Mom
told it to me. It takes a
lot longer than 30 min. at 350°.
I think it could use a little
higher temperature.)

(Mrs. Frank Reynolds) Chocolate Pie

3 c sugar
Pinch salt
4 eggs
1 t vanilla
1 large canned milk
7 T cocoa
1 stick margarine, melted
2 c flaked coconut

Mix sugar, salt and cocoa together. Add eggs and mix well. Stir in vanilla and milk. Add melted margarine, then coconut. Pour into 2 unbaked pie shells. (If frozen crusts are used, it will make 3.)

Bake in a 350° oven about 40 min or until firm. A cup of nuts for each pie may be added, if desired.

Peach Cobbler

1 c flour
1 c sugar
1 t baking powder
½ t salt
¾ c milk
1 stick margarine

Melt margarine in baking dish and pour in above mixture. Do not stir Mix ¾ c sugar with about 10 sliced peaches. Pour over batter mixture. Do not stir. Bake at 350° for about 40 min.

Pineapple Chess Pie

Cream together
  1 box light brown sugar
  2 T flour
  1 stick margarine

Add
  3 eggs
  1 small can crushed pineapple
  1 T vanilla

Set oven at 450° then
turn back to 350° to bake
pies.
  Pour mixture into two
unbaked 9 in pie shells.
Bake until done – about
30 min –

  Makes 2 pies.

Frances and Walter Murphy, Formal Portrait

Plain Pastry (Pie Crust)

4 T fat (Crisco)
1 c flour
¼ t baking powder
½ t salt
¼ c water (or less)

Cut fat into flour, baking powder and salt. Add enough cold water to hold dough together but not sticky. Makes one crust.

Possum Pie #1

3 egg whites
¾ c sugar
1 c chocolate wafer crumbs
        or 20 Ritz crackers
½ c nuts
½ t vanilla

Beat eggs. Add sugar gradually. Add other ingredients. Bake 325°. for 25 min. in sprayed pan. Let set in refrigerator to mellow.

Possum Pie #2

30 Ritz crackers, crushed
1 c chopped nuts
3 egg whites
1 c sugar
½ c heavy cream, whipped
Grated coconut

Combine crackers and nuts. Beat egg whites until frothy and gradually add sugar. Beat until stiff. Fold crackers and nuts into egg whites. Turn mixture into lightly greased pie pan. Bake in 350° oven for 15 min. or until lightly browned. Cool.

Just before serving, top with whipped cream and sprinkle with coconut.

Makes 6 servings

Quick Cobbler

½ c flour
Pinch of salt
½ c sugar
1 t baking powder

Mix together and add ½ c milk and mix well. Add 2 c peaches (or any other fruit such as cherries, strawberries, blueberries, etc) Pour in casserole dish. Dot with butter. Bake 350° for about 35-45 min. or until crust comes to top and browns.

Quick Coconut Cream Pie

1 5.1oz instant vanilla pudding
1½ c cold milk
8 oz Cool Whip, divided
¾ to 1 c flaked coconut, divided
       and toasted if desired
1 baked or Graham cracker crust

In mixing bowl, beat pudding and milk for 2 min. Fold in ½ Cool Whip and ½ to ¾ c coconut. Pour into crust. Spread with remaining Cool Whip and sprinkle with remaining coconut. Chill.

6 - 8 servings

(Rachel Cahill's) Coconut Cream Pie

3 c milk
1 c sugar
5 T corn starch
3 eggs (separated)

½ stick butter
1 t vanilla
1 c coconut
cooked pie crust

Scald milk in saucepan. Combine sugar and cornstarch and add vanilla to scalded milk — stir continuously until mixture begins to thicken. Divide eggs reserving whites for meringue. Beat egg yolks in small bowl and add the hot mixture to yolks to temper them. Then add yolk mixture to saucepan and continue stirring until custard is thick. Add butter and vanilla — mix well. Add ¾ cup coconut. Cool before pouring into cooked pie crust. Toast ¼ c coconut for top of meringue. Meringue — Add 1 T cold water to egg whites. Beat until loose peaks form. Add 6 T sugar and beat until stiff peaks form. Bake in 350° preheated oven for 10 min. Remove and add toasted coconut.

Good!!

Shoney's Strawberry Pie

1 baked 9 in pie shell

3/4 c sugar
1 c water
1/4 t salt
2 T cornstarch
1/4 of 3 oz strawberry gelatin
2-3 drops red food coloring
1 qt. strawberries
whipped cream or Cool Whip

Combine sugar, water, salt and cornstarch in saucepan; cook, stirring, until clear and thickened.

Remove from heat; add gelatin, stir until dissolved. Add coloring. Cool. Pour over berries in pie shell. Refrigerate. Cover with whipped cream or Cool Whip.

Sliced Sweet Potato Pie

2-3 sweet potatoes
1 c brown sugar
1 c white sugar
1 t nutmeg
1 t vanilla
1 t cinnamon
1 c scalded milk
Pinch of butter for each layer

Boil sweet potatoes. Peel and cut into slices 1/4 in thick. Mix sugars with nutmeg and cinnamon. Put potatoes in layers in crust with mixture of sugar and spices. Dot each layer with butter. Add vanilla to scalded milk then pour over potatoes. Cover with top crust. Bake in slow oven 325° for about an hour,

Sweet Potato Pie

2 eggs, well-beaten
2 c sugar
1 large can evaporated milk
2 c cooked sweet potatoes
1 stick margarine, melted
1 t vanilla
1 t lemon flavoring
¼ t salt

Beat together eggs and sugar well. Add about ½ the milk and continue beating. Add the rest of the milk and finish beating, making sure sugar is dissolved. Fold in sweet potatoes, melted margarine, flavorings and salt. Place mixture in pie shells. Bake 45 min. at 350°. Makes 2 9 in. pies.

Toddle House Butterscotch Cream Pie

1 4 serving size butterscotch pudding mix
2 c milk
2 T brown sugar
¼ c butter, melted to golden brown
¼ t vanilla
1 Baked pie shell
½ c heavy cream, whipped

Prepare pudding mix by package directions, using 2 c milk. Add brown sugar, butter and vanilla. Cover surface of pudding with waxed paper. Chill. Beat with a spoon until smooth. Pour into pie shell. Top with whipped cream.

Toddle House Chocolate Pie

2½ c + 2 T sugar
½ c + 6 T cornstarch
½ c cocoa
¾ t salt
1½ pints sweet milk
2½ egg yolks
¾ t vanilla
Baked pie shells
Whipped cream

Sift together sugar, cornstarch, cocoa and salt into mixer bowl. At med. speed add ½ the milk and mix thoroughly. Add egg yolks; mix well, being careful that the mixture does not foam. Scald remaining milk and add to chocolate mix. Stir with wooden spoon and cook until consistency of whipped cream. Put in bowl of mixer on medium. Allow to mix. Cool. Add vanilla and allow to mix for 5 min. Cover with wax paper and completely cool before placing in refrigerator. Use 1½ ll of filling in each pie shell. Top with whipped cream. Should make 2 - 3 pies.

Salads

Alice Johnson's Frozen Banana Salad

6 oz cream cheese
1/2 t salt
2 T mayonnaise
1 T lemon juice
1/2 c drained crushed pineapple
1/2 c chopped maraschino cherries
1/2 c nuts
1 c heavy cream
2 c mashed ripe bananas (3 to 4)

Soften cheese with a fork. Add salt, mayonnaise and lemon juice. Mix well. Fold in pineapple, cherries and nuts. Whip cream and fold into cheese mixture. Add bananas. Turn into molds or freezing tray and freeze until firm. Makes 8 - 10 servings.

(Put foil over tray or molds to keep ice crystals from forming on top.)

Apple Salad

3 celery ribs, finely chopped
4 med apples, peeled and chopped
1 c Cool Whip
1/4 c chopped dates or raisins
2 T chopped pecans
4 t mayonnaise

Combine all ingredients Cover and refrigerate until serving.

6 servings

Becky Hedrick's Salad

1 6oz orange Jello } dissolve
1 c boiling water
1 c orange and pineapple juice } add
1 c cold water
3 oz cream cheese (melt in hot mix)
add
1 can crushed pineapple, drained
1 can mandarin oranges, drained
4 small shredded carrots
½ c chopped pecans
1 c miniature marshmallows

Topping
8 oz Cool Whip
½ c mayonnaise
Sprinkle Cheddar cheese on top

Makes 9 X 13 in. pan
Good with ham or turkey.

Betty Carriker's Sauerkraut Salad

2 c sauerkraut, drained
½ c sugar
Combine and mix well. Let stand
30 min -
Add
½ c thinly sliced celery
½ c chopped green pepper
½ c grated carrots
½ c chopped onion
2 oz. chopped pimento, drained

Stir well. Cover and chill at
least 12 hrs. (24 is better.)

Broccoli - Carrot Salad

1½ c broccoli flowerets, blanched
1 med. red apple, chopped
1 med. carrot, grated
¼ c raisins
Dressing
½ c mayonnaise
2 T vinegar
¼ t salt
⅛ t pepper

In salad bowl, combine salad ingredients. In a small bowl, with fork, mix dressing ingredients. Pour over salad. Toss until coated. Line serving dish with lettuce leaves; spoon salad on top.

4 servings

Carrot - Pineapple Salad

8 oz crushed pineapple
3 oz lemon Jello
1 c boiling water
½ c cold water
1 t white vinegar
⅛ t salt
2 med. carrots, grated

Drain pineapple. Reserve ½ c. Dissolve Jello in boiling water. Stir in cold water, vinegar, salt and reserved juice. Chill until partially thickened (about 45 min). Stir in carrots and pineapple. Pour in 3 cup mold coated with non stick spray. Chill until firm. Unmold.

4 servings

Carrot - Raisin Salad

3/4 lb carrots, scraped and shredded
1/4 C + 2T raisins
1/4 C + 2T chopped nuts
1/2 c mayonnaise
1 1/2 T cider vinegar
1 T sugar
1/8 t lemon juice

Combine carrots, raisins and nuts in a bowl. Combine remaining ingredients, stir well; add to carrot mixture. Toss gently.

Yield: 4 servings

Cherry Coke Salad

1 20 oz crushed pineapple
1/2 c water
6 oz cherry gelatin
1 can cherry pie filling
3/4 c cola

Drain pineapple, reserving juice; set fruit aside. In a saucepan bring pineapple juice and water to a boil. Add gelatin; stir until dissolved. Stir in pie filling and cola. Pour into serving bowl. Refrigerate until slightly thickened. Fold in reserved pineapple. Refrigerate until firm.

Yield: 10-12 servings

Chicken Salad on Cantaloupe Rings

2½ c cubed cooked chicken
1 c sliced celery
1 c halved green grapes
2 T minced fresh parsley
½ c mayonnaise
1 T lemon juice

1 T vinegar
1½ t prepared mustard
½ t salt
½ t sugar
⅛ t pepper
4 cantaloupe rings

In a large bowl, combine chicken, celery, grapes and parsley. Combine the next seven ingredients; mix well. Pour over chicken mixture and toss. Chill for at least 1 hour. To serve, place 1 c of chicken salad on each cantaloupe ring; sprinkle with almonds.

Yield 4 servings

Cranberry Pineapple Freeze

1 can whole cranberry sauce
1 can pineapple tidbits
2-3 sliced bananas
½ c chopped nuts
1 Cool Whip (large)

Combine ingredients; spread in baking pan or freezer container or mold and freeze. To serve cut into squares.

Can serve as salad or dessert

Cranberry Pineapple Salad
(Taste of Home Magazine)

6 oz raspberry Jello
1 3/4 c boiling water
1 16 oz jellied cranberry sauce
1 8 oz crushed pineapple, undrained
3/4 c orange juice
1 T lemon juice
1/2 c chopped nuts

Dissolve Jello in boiling water. Break up and stir in cranberry sauce. Add pineapple, orange juice and lemon juice. Chill until partially set. Stir in nuts. Pour into 7 x 11 in dish. Chill until firm.

Serves 12

Cranberry Salad

1 1/2 c sugar
1 c boiling water
1 3 oz cherry Jello
Small can crushed pineapple
1 1/2 c ground fresh cranberries
Ground rind of 1 orange
1/2 c chopped nuts
Diced sections of 1 orange

Add boiling water to Jello. After this has partly congealed, mix well with other ingredients which have been thoroughly blended. Pour into mold and let stand until firm.

Crown Jewel Salad Cake

Prepare one 3 oz orange, cherry and lime flavor Jello separately, dissolving each in 1 c boiling water and adding ½ c cold water. Pour each flavor into a separate 8 in square pan. Chill till firm at least 3 hours. Cut into ½ in cubes. Set aside a few cubes for garnish.

Dissolve 3 oz lemon Jello and ¼ c sugar in 1 c boiling water; add ½ c pineapple juice. Chill until slightly thickened. Blend in 4 cups Cool Whip and the Jello cubes. Spoon into a 9 in spring-form pan. Chill overnight or until firm. Run a spatula around sides of pan; gently remove sides. Garnish with reserved cubes.

Makes 16 servings

Doris Ammon's Cranberry Salad

1 3 oz cherry Jello
1 c hot water
1 c sugar
1 T lemon juice
1 c pineapple juice

1 c ground raw cranberries
1 ground orange
1 can crushed pineapple, drained
1 c ground celery
½ c ground nuts

Dissolve Jello. Add sugar, lemon juice and pineapple juice. Let cool. Add other ingredients. Put in mold.

Dreamy Frozen Fruit Salad

1 8 oz whipped topping
6 oz cream cheese, softened
¼ c lemon juice
1 can sweetened condensed milk
1 c chopped pecans
1 pineapple chunks, drained
1 cherry pie filling

Combine cream cheese and lemon juice; beat until smooth. Stir in milk, pecans and pineapple. Fold in whipped topping and pie filling. Place about 24 paper baking cups in muffin tins; spoon mixture into cups. Cover and freeze.

Yield: about 24 servings

Frances Storey's Pea Salad

1 c cheddar cheese – cubed small
1 large onion, cut fine
8-9 Gerkin sweet pickles –
        chopped fine
3 ribs celery finely chopped
1 can green peas, drained

Mix dressing and above ingredients well.

Dressing

½ c mayonnaise
2 t Dijohn mustard
1 T sugar
2 T vinegar

Frosted Lime Walnut Salad

3 oz lime gelatin
1 c boiling water
1 20 oz crushed pineapple
1 c small curd cottage cheese

½ c chopped celery
1 T chopped pimento
½ c chopped walnuts

Dissolve gelatin in boiling water; cool till syrupy. Stir in remaining ingredients. Mold in 8 in square pan rinsed in cold water.

Frosting – When salad is firm, unmold or leave in pan. Frost top with 1 3 oz cream cheese mixed with 1 T mayonnaise and 1 t lemon juice, Decorate with maraschino cherries, watercress and walnut halves.

Makes 6 – 9 servings

Fiftieth Anniversary

Fruit and Juice Squares

1½ c boiling water
6 oz cherry Jello
1 c orange juice and ice cubes
1 can fruit cocktail, drained
1 8 oz Cool Whip, divided

Dissolve Jello in boiling water.
Mix cold juice and ice to make
1½ cups. Stir into Jello. Refrigerate
30 min. or until slightly
thickened. Remove 1½ c of the
Jello; stir in fruit.
Stir ½ of the Cool Whip into
remaining Jello with wire
whisk until blended. Pour
into 8 in. square dish. Refrigerate
about 10 min. until set but
not firm. Carefully spoon
fruited Jello over creamy
layer in dish.
Refrigerate 3 hrs. or until firm.
Cut into squares. Garnish with
remaining Cool Whip.
Makes 9 servings

Fruited Lemon Jello Salad

6 oz lemon Jello
2 c boiling water
12 oz lemon-lime soda
20 oz crushed pineapple
15 g mandarin oranges, drained
2 C halved green grapes

1 egg
½ c sugar
2 T flour
1 T margarine
1 c whipping cream, whipped

Dissolve Jello in boiling water. Stir in soda. Refrigerate until partially set. Drain pineapple; reserve juice. Add water to pineapple juice to make 1 cup; set aside. Stir pineapple, oranges and grapes into Jello. Pour into 9 X 13 in. dish. Refrigerate. In saucepan over medium heat, combine egg, sugar, flour, butter and reserved pineapple juice. Bring to a boil; cook and stir 2 min. or until thickened. Cool completely. Fold in whipped cream. Spread over Jello. Refrigerate until firm. Cut into squares.

Yield: 15-18 servings

Heavenly Salad

1 20 oz crushed pineapple, undrained
1 4 oz instant banana pudding mix

Pour pineapple over pudding and add
1 c fresh fruit or fruit cocktail
1 diced banana
½ c coconut
1 c miniature marshmallows
1 c chopped maraschino cherries
½ c chopped nuts
1 carton Cool Whip

Mix all ingredients and refrigerate. Makes a good salad or dessert.

Holiday Ribbon Salad

6 oz lime Jello
5 c boiling water, divided
4 c cold water, divided
1 3 oz lemon Jello
½ c miniature marshmallows

1 8 oz cream cheese, softened
1 c mayonnaise
1 8 oz crushed pineapple, undrained
6 oz cherry Jello

In a bowl, dissolve lime Jello in 2 c boiling water. Add 2 c cold water; stir. Pour into 9 x 13 in dish; refrigerate until set, about 1 hour.

In a bowl, dissolve lemon Jello in 1 c boiling water. Stir in marshmallows until melted. Cool 20 min. In a small bowl, beat cream cheese and mayonnaise until smooth. Gradually beat in lemon Jello. Stir in pineapple. Carefully spoon over the lime layer. Chill until set.

Dissolve cherry Jello in 2 cups boiling water. Add remaining cold water; stir. Spoon over the lemon layer. Refrigerate overnight. Cut into squares.

Yield 12 - 15 servings

Lime Gelatin Salad

6 oz lime Jello
1 c boiling water
8 oz. cream cheese
½ t vanilla
15 oz mandarine oranges,
        drained

8 oz crushed pineapple, drained
1 c lemon-lime soda
½ c pecans, chopped
8 oz Cool Whip, divided

Dissolve Jello in water. In a mixing bowl, beat cream cheese until fluffy. Stir in Jello mixture and beat until smooth. Stir in vanilla, oranges, pineapple, soda and pecans. Chill until mixture mounds slightly when dropped from a spoon. Fold in ¾ of the Cool Whip. Pour into a 9 X 13 in dish. Refrigerate for 3-4 hours or until firm. Cut into squares. Garnish with the remaining Cool Whip.

Yield: 16 - 20 servings

Lime Party Salad

¼ lb marshmallows
1 c milk
1 3oz lime Jello
6 oz cream cheese
1 20oz crushed pineapple, undrained
1 c heavy cream, whipped
⅔ c mayonnaise
½ c chopped nuts

Combine marshmallows and milk in top of double boiler. Heat, stirring, until marshmallows are melted and mixture is smooth. Use this hot mixture to dissolve Jello. Blend Jello mixture into softened cream cheese, which has been whipped until fluffy.

Add pineapple; blend in and allow to cool to room temperature. Fold in whipped cream, mayonnaise and nuts. Pour into molds or a glass dish 9 x 11 in. Chill until firm.

Makes 6 or more servings

Marjorie Petrou's Vegetable Salad

1 17 oz small English peas, drained
1 17 oz white shoepeg corn, drained
1 15 oz French style green beans, drained
1 4 oz jar chopped pimento
½ c celery, chopped
1 c onion, chopped
1 green pepper, chopped
Dressing
　1 c sugar
　½ c oil
　¾ c vinegar
　1 t salt
　½ t pepper

Combine vegetables. Toss lightly.
Combine sugar, oil, vinegar,
salt and pepper in a sauce pan.
Bring to a boil over low heat.
Pour over vegetables. Stir
gently to blend. Cover and
chill 12 to 24 hours.
　　　　　　　　　　Good!

Menu suggestion - Serve with chicken
salad, fruits and rolls. Makes a
good meal.

Marlene Johnson's Broccoli Salad

1 bunch broccoli and/or cauliflower
  (I use half of each)
1 med. onion
½ c raisins
½ c sunflower seed
bacon bits, if desired

Chop broccoli and/or cauliflower
and onion fine

Mix with sauce as follows:
  ½ c mayonnaise
  1 T vinegar
  2 T sugar

Let set overnight for
added flavor.

Good!

Mom Kite's Pineapple Salad

Heat juice drained from
20 oz crushed pineapple. Dissolve
3 oz pack lemon jello in juice.
Add 1 c miniature marshmallows.
Stir until mix begins to jell.
Whip 1 c whipping cream and add.
Add 1 c cottage cheese, pineapple
and ½ jar maraschino cherries
that have been chopped. Add
nuts if desired. Pour into
mold. Refrigerate until ready
to serve.

(For Christmas - add red
and green cherries)

Mrs. Grunert's Cherry Salad
(Louise Leonard's Mother)

1 3 oz cherry Jello
1 can sour red pie cherries
½ c chopped pecans
½ c sugar

Drain and chop cherries. Add sugar and cook 2 min. Add to Jello dissolved in juice from cherries adding water to make 1 cup. Mix and pour in mold.

Noel Salad Loaf

Blend 8 oz cream cheese and ⅓ c mayonnaise; add ½ c chopped celery, 1 c crushed pineapple, drained. Whip 1 c whipping cream; fold in. Tint pink with food coloring. Cube ¾ of a 1 lb can of jellied cranberry sauce; add. Freeze in loaf pan.

Serves 8

Peach Relish Salad

1 3oz lime Jello
1½ c boiling water
1 T vinegar
¼ t salt
½ c mayonnaise
½ c diced celery
3 T sweet pickle relish
2 c diced fresh peaches

Dissolve Jello in hot water. Blend in cold water, vinegar and salt. Cool until slightly thickened. Add mayonnaise and beat with egg beater until fluffy. Fold in celery, pickle relish and peach slices which have been diced. Turn into 1 qt. mold or individual molds and chill until firm. Unmold and garnish with greens and additional peach slices.

Makes 6 individual molds

Pet and Opal's Salad

8 oz cottage cheese
1 3oz orange Jello
Sprinkle Jello on cheese and
mix well with your hand.
Add 4oz Cool Whip
Then add 1 (303 size) can mandarin
    oranges drained and cut in half
Add 15½ oz pineapple tidbits, drained
Mix well.

    Can add a few nuts and/
or marachino cherries.

Pet's Salad

1 3oz lime or orange Jello
1 c water
1 can crushed pineapple, undrained
1 c sour cream

Optional   few nuts
             few marshmallow

    Mix all together.

Pineapple Gelatin Salad

1 20oz crushed pineapple
1 6oz lemon Jello
3 c boiling water
1 8oz cream cheese, softened
1 16oz Cool Whip

¾ c sugar
3 T lemon juice
3 T water
2 T flour
2 egg yolks, beaten

Drain pineapple; reserve juice. Dissolve Jello in water; add pineapple. Pour into a 9x13in dish; chill until almost set, about 45 min. In a mixing bowl, beat cream cheese and whipped topping until smooth. Carefully spread over gelatin; chill 30 min. Meanwhile, in a saucepan over medium heat, combine sugar, lemon juice, water, flour, egg yolks and reserved pineapple juice; bring to a boil, stirring constantly. Cook 1 min or until thickened. Cool. Carefully spread over cream cheese layer. Chill at least 1 hour.

Yield: 12-16 servings

Pineapple - Orange Salad

1 15½ oz crushed pineapple, undrained
1 6 oz orange Jello
2 c buttermilk
1 c flaked coconut
1 c chopped nuts
1 12 oz Cool Whip

Place pineapple in sauce pan; bring to a boil, stirring constantly. Remove from heat. Add Jello, stirring until dissolved. Stir in buttermilk, coconut and pecans, cool. Fold in whipped topping; pour into a 9 x 13 in dish. Chill until firm.

Yield: 15 servings

Pink Arctic Freeze

6 oz cream cheese
2 T mayonnaise
2 T sugar
1 whole cranberry sauce
1 c crushed pineapple, drained
½ c chopped nuts
1 c whipping cream, whipped

Soften cheese; blend in mayonnaise and sugar. Add fruits and nuts. Fold in whipped cream. Pour into 8½ x 4½ x 2½ in. loaf pan. Freeze firm 6 hrs. or overnight. To serve let stand at room temperature about 15 min; turn out on lettuce and slice.

Makes 8 – 10 servings

(can add a little red cake color.)

Pink Fruit Freeze

1 8 oz cream cheese
1 qt Cherry ice cream, softened
½ c Miracle Whip
2 18 oz fruit cocktail, drained
⅓ c chopped nuts

Combine softened cream cheese, ice cream and salad dressing, mixing until well blended. Fold in fruit and nuts. Pour into 9 in square pan. Freeze until firm. Place in refrigerator 15 min. before serving. Cut into squares. Garnish with cherries, mint and holly leaves, if desired.

Makes 9 servings

Pretzel Salad

Bottom:
  1 stick melted butter
  ½ c sugar
  1 c crushed pretzels
Combine ingredients and press
into pan.

Middle
  1 8 oz cream cheese
  1 8 oz Cool Whip
  ½ c sugar
  Put in bowl and mix with
mixer.

Top
  1 20 oz crushed pineapple, undrained
  2 T corn starch
  Boil 2 min and spread
on top.

Ruth Church's Cranberry Salad

  1 6 oz cherry Jello
  2 c boiling water
  1 can whole-berry cranberry sauce
  1 20 oz crushed pineapple, drained
  1 c orange juice
  1 c chopped pecans
  (can use juice drained from
    pineapple as part of 2 c water.)

  Dissolve Jello in boiling liquid.
Add remaining ingredients. Be
sure cranberry sauce is mixed
well. Pour into mold sprayed
with non-stick spray, chill
until firm.

  Serves 10 - 12

Stuffed Celery Trunks

1 c (4 oz) shredded Cheddar cheese
½ c mayonnaise
2 T chopped pimento-stuffed olives
6 stalks celery, cut into 4 in pieces

Combine first 3 ingredients, mixing well. Stuff celery pieces with cheese mixture.

Yield: 1 dozen

Sunny Carrot Salad

3 c shredded carrots
2 c crushed pineapple, drained
½ c golden raisins
⅓ c mayonnaise
½ c sliced almonds
⅓ c sunflower kernels

In a large serving bowl, combine the carrots, pineapple and raisins. Stir in mayonnaise. Cover and refrigerate until serving. Just before serving, add almonds and sunflower kernels; toss to coat.

Yield: 5 servings

The Butner's Angel's Delight Salad

add {
6 oz cream cheese ⟩ mix
4 T mayonnaise ⟩
1 can crushed pineapple, drained
1 can fruit cocktail, drained
1 c chopped nuts
½ lb miniature marshmallows

Add 1 pint cream, whipped
(I only use ½ pt or a
carton of Cool Whip works
just as well.)

Mix well and freeze in
molds or cup cake liners.

(This is what I often make
at Christmas but I add
some green cake color
to it.)

Turkey Waldorf Salad

¼ c mayonnaise
3 T sour cream
1 T lemon juice
¼ t salt
¼ t black pepper
2 c cubed Red Delicious apples
1½ c cubed cooked turkey breast
1 c seedless red grapes, halved
½ c diced celery
2 T chopped nuts, toasted

Combine first 5 ingredients. Stir with a whisk. Combine apple, turkey, grapes, celery and nuts in a bowl. Stir Stir in mayonnaise mixture, cover and chill.

5 servings

Watergate Salad

mix {
1 instant pistachio pudding mix
1 20oz crushed pineapple, undrained
1 8oz Cool Whip
1 c miniature marshmallows
½ c chopped nuts

Mix pudding and pineapple together. Add Cool Whip, marshmallows and nuts. Refrigerate.

Soups

Amish Cheesy Chicken Chowder

3 c chicken broth
2 c diced peeled potatoes
1 c diced carrots
1 c diced celery
½ c diced onion
1½ t salt

¼ t pepper
¼ c butter, cubed
⅓ c flour
2 c milk
2 c shredded cheddar cheese
2 c diced cooked chicken

In a 4 qt. saucepan, bring chicken broth to a boil. Reduce heat; add vegetables, salt and pepper. Cover and simmer for 12-15 min. or until vegetables are tender.

Meanwhile, melt butter in med. pan; stir in flour until smooth. Gradually stir in milk. Bring to a boil over med. heat; cook and stir 2 min. or until thickened. Reduce heat; add cheese, stirring until melted; add to broth along with chicken. Cook and stir until heated through.

Yield: 6-8 servings

Good !!!

Cheesy Chicken Chowder

1 chopped onion	4 T butter
1 c chopped carrots	6 T flour
1 c diced potatoes	2 c milk
1 c diced celery	1 c shredded Cheddar cheese
4 c water	1 t salt
5 c diced cooked chicken	

Combine vegetables and water in a soup pot and bring to a boil; reduce heat to med. and cook until soft, about 20 min.

Add chicken and butter. Stir in the flour, then gradually stir in the milk.

Add the cheese and salt and stir until the cheese is melted.

Spoon into bowls and serve.

Serves 4 – 6

Murph's 90th Birthday

Chicken and Potato Chowder

¼ c butter

1 onion, diced

3 carrots, diced

2 stalks celery, diced

1 t thyme

¼ c flour

3 c chicken broth

2 c milk - more if needed

2 russet potatoes, peeled + cubed

2 c diced cooked chicken, breast

1½ c shredded sharp Cheddar cheese

salt and pepper, to taste

2 T chopped fresh parsley

Melt butter in large pot over med. heat. Add onion, celery and carrots. Cook, stirring occasionally, about 3-4 min. Stir in thyme until fragrant, about 1 min.

Whisk in flour until lightly browned, about 1 min. Gradually whisk in broth and milk; cook, whisking constantly until slightly thickened, about 1-2 min. Stir in potatoes. Bring to a boil; reduce heat and simmer until potatoes are tender, about 12-15 min. Stir in chicken and cheese, gradually, until smooth, about 1-2 min. Season with salt and pepper to taste. If chowder is too thick, add more milk until desired consistency. Serve immediately. Garnish with parsley.

Serves 6

Cream of Broccoli Soup

2 c water
4 t chicken bouillon granules
2 10 oz frozen chopped broccoli
2 T finely chopped onion
2 cans cream of chicken soup, undiluted
2 c evaporated milk
2 16 oz sour cream
1 t dried parsley flakes
¼ t pepper

In large saucepan, combine water and bouillon. Add broccoli and onion. Bring to a boil; reduce heat. Simmer for 10 min or until broccoli is crisp tender. Combine soup, milk, sour cream, parsley and pepper. Add to broccoli mixture. Cook and stir for 3-5 min. or until heated through.

Yield : 6-8 servings

Cream of Peanut Soup

2 stalks celery, chopped
1 small onion, chopped
¼ c butter
¼ c flour
2 c chicken broth
1 c milk
1 c light cream
1 c peanut butter
Salt and pepper to taste
Watercress for garnish

Brown celery and onion in butter. Stir in flour and gradually add chicken broth. Add milk and cream; strain. Stir in peanut butter and simmer for 5 min. Season with salt and pepper. Garnish with chopped peanuts and a sprig of watercress.

Serves 8

Slow Cooker

Homemade Vegetable Soup

1 lb. stewing meat, cut into pieces
1 bay leaf
1 small onion, diced
2 ribs celery, sliced
2-3 potatoes, diced
14½ oz can stewed tomatoes
8 oz can tomato sauce
¼ c frozen corn   *
½ c frozen green beans *
¼ c frozen peas   *
¼ c chopped cabbage
salt and pepper to taste

Combine all ingredients
in cooker. Add water to
fill pot.
Cover. Cook on low 6-8 hours

Serves 10-12

* I would use a bag of mixed
frozen vegetables. It would be
easier!

Louise Smith's Quick Old-Fashioned Soup

½ lb ground beef
1 can (10½ oz) beef bouillon
1 can (10½ oz) onion soup
2 cans (8 oz) tomato sauce
1 can (8 oz) lima or butter beans
1 can (8 oz) green beans
1 can (16 oz) peas and carrots
½ bag (1 lb) frozen potatoes or
    1 can (10½ oz) potato soup
Seasoned salt, pepper, garlic salt
    and celery salt to taste

Cook meat in a skillet, stirring, until red color is gone. If needed to prevent sticking, add a small amount of oil. Diced, cooked leftover beef roast can be substituted for ground beef.

Add remaining ingredients except seasonings; simmer 30 min. Season to taste.

Mom Krites' Chili Con Carne

2 quarts tomatoes
1 lb hamburger
1 big onion, chopped
½ pod green pepper, chopped
1 can kidney beans, drained, rinsed
½ c elbow macaroni
salt and pepper to taste

Brown beef and onion; pour into all the other ingredients. Rinse pan with a little water and add it also. Bring to a boil. Drop in macaroni. Simmer for about ½ hour. Put a wire "rack" (like you put under a glass coffee pot) under it and it won't stick as badly.

Good!

Old Timey Potato Soup

1 medium onion, minced
¼ c butter
4 c diced raw potatoes
2 c water
1 t salt
4 c milk
Few dashes of celery seed
Salt and pepper to taste
4 slices bacon, cooked and
     crumbled (optional)

Saute onion in butter until translucent. Add potatoes, water and salt and cook until tender. Add milk and season to taste. Simmer a few minutes before serving.

Potato Cheese Soup

2 c diced raw potatoes
3 T chopped onion
3 c water
3 T margarine
¼ c flour
1 t salt
¼ t pepper
1 c grated cheese
1½ - 2 c milk

Cook potatoes and onion in water. Do not drain. In another pan, melt margarine; stir in flour, salt, pepper, cheese and milk. Cook until thickened. Add cheese sauce to potatoes and onions. (If soup is too thin, add a few instant potatoes.) Do not boil.

Makes about 4 big bowls

Good!

Pumpkin Soup

6 c low-sodium chicken broth (48 oz)
1 29 oz can pumpkin purée
1 med onion chopped (1 c)
1 clove garlic, minced
1 t chopped fresh thyme or ½ t dried
1½ t salt or to taste
⅛ t black pepper
½ c heavy cream

Bring first 7 ingredients to boil in a large pot over high heat. Reduce heat to low and simmer 15 to 30 min. uncovered. Purée soup 2 c at a time in a blender or food processor. Return to pot and stir into cream and if desired, thin soup with additional broth or water. You can add a little brown sugar to taste if you like. Pour into bowls and garnish with parsley.

Serves 8

Vegetable Beef Soup

1 lb. stew beef cut in cubes
1 large onion, chopped
1 (14 oz) can or 1½ c fresh corn (3 ears)
1 (14 oz) can lima beans or 1½ c fresh
1 (8 oz) tomato sauce
1 c sliced carrots
1 c thinly sliced okra
1 c diced potatoes
½ c sliced celery
salt to taste
black pepper - optional
1 (28 oz) can tomatoes or 2½ c fresh

Cook beef and onion in 1 quart water until beef is tender. Add vegetables. Add salt to taste and pepper if desired. Simmer over medium-low heat until vegetables are tender.

Vegetables

Asparagus Casserole

1 No. 2 cans asparagus spears
4 hard cooked eggs
1 can cream of asparagus soup
½ lb grated cheese
¾ c almonds
Seasoned salt
Buttered bread crumbs

Drain asparagus and reserve liquid. Arrange half the spears in the bottom of a small casserole. Cover with 2 sliced hard cooked eggs, ¼ lb. cheese and some almonds. Repeat layers. Blend asparagus liquid with soup and pour into casserole. Sprinkle with seasoned salt and top with buttered bread crumbs. Heat in a 400° oven for 20-25 min. or until lightly browned and bubbly.

Makes 6 servings

Au Gratin Potato Casserole

1 (32 oz) frozen hash browns, thawed
1 (16 oz) sour cream
2 c (8 oz) shredded cheddar cheese
1 (10¾ oz) cream of mushroom soup
1 small onion, chopped
¼ t pepper

2 c crushed cornflakes
¼ c margarine, melted

Stir together first 6 ingredients in a large bowl. Spoon mix into a lightly greased 13×9 in baking dish. Sprinkle evenly with cornflakes and drizzle with margarine.
Bake 325° for 1 hr. 20 min. or until bubbly.

Makes 10 - 12 servings

Baked Cranberry Sauce

1 lb cranberries
1 c flaked coconut
¾ c sugar
1½ c chopped pecans
½ c water

Combine all ingredients. Pour into a greased 11×7 in. dish. Bake, uncovered, 25 - 30 min. or until berries are tender. Serve warm or cold. Refrigerate leftovers.

Makes 10 servings

Baked Shredded Carrots

6 c shredded carrots (about 2 lbs.)
¾ c chopped green onion
2 T sugar
½ t salt
½ t celery salt
¼ c butter

In a large bowl, combine carrots, onions, sugar, salt and celery salt. Transfer to an ungreased 1½ qt. baking dish. Dot with butter. Cover and bake at 325° for 40 - 45 min. or until carrots are crisp tender.

Yield: 6 servings

Barbecue Slaw

1 small head cabbage, grated
2 stalks celery, finely chopped
1 med. green pepper, finely chopped
½ c chopped onion
¾ c tomato ketchup
¼ c vinegar
2 T sugar
1 T Worcestershire sauce
1 T prepared mustard
1 t salt
Dash cayenne pepper or hot pepper sauce

Combine first 4 ingredients in bowl. Combine ketchup and remaining ingredients. Toss with vegetables. Cover and chill for several hours.

Makes about 1 quart

Barbecue slaw will keep for several weeks in a covered container in the refrigerator.

Betty Huff's Sweet Potato Casserole

1 large can sweet potatoes (drain)
1 large can crushed pineapple
1 c sugar
1 c raisins
1 small can black walnuts

Mash potatoes. Add sugar and mash again. Add pineapple, raisins and black walnuts.

Put in a casserole dish. Sprinkle with brown sugar and dot with butter. Heat in 325° oven for half an hour.

Broccoli Casserole

2 (10oz) chopped broccoli
1 c grated cheese
1 c mayonnaise
1 c mushroom soup
2 eggs, beaten
1 small onion, chopped
1 c crushed crackers

Cook broccoli 5 min.; drain. Mix ingredients together and put in baking dish. Top with crackers. Bake at 350° for 30 min.

Serves 8-10

Broccoli - Pea Casserole

2 (10 oz) frozen chopped broccoli
1 (303) can green peas
1 (10½ oz) cream of mushroom soup
1 c mayonnaise
1 t salt
½ t pepper
1 c shredded sharp Cheddar cheese
1 med. onion, chopped
2 eggs, beaten
½ c crushed buttery crackers

Cook broccoli according to package directions. Drain. Arrange half of broccoli in greased 2 qt. casserole dish. Cover with peas. Mix soup, mayonnaise, salt, pepper, cheese, onion and eggs to make a sauce. Pour ½ of sauce over broccoli and peas. Add the rest of the broccoli and top with remaining sauce. Sprinkle crushed crackers on top.
Bake 350° for 30 min.
Serves 8

Cabbage Au Gratin

2 1/2 c cooked cabbage
3 T butter
3 T flour
3/4 c evaporated milk
3/4 c water from cabbage
Salt to taste
1 c grated cheese
1/2 c dry corn bread crumbles
2 T butter, melted

Drain cabbage and save water. Melt butter. Blend in flour. Add evaporated milk and water drained from cabbage. Stir until thickened.

In oven safe dish, layer cabbage, sauce, cheese. Repeat with all ingredients and add cornbread crumbles mixed with butter. Bake 350° until it bubbles and is hot through and through.

(Can add onion if desired)

Carrot Casserole

2 lb. carrots, cooked and mashed
½ c milk
½ c sugar
⅓ c margarine, melted
2 eggs, beaten
1 t vanilla

Topping
⅔ c packed brown sugar
⅓ c flour
2 T cold margarine
⅔ c chopped pecans
⅔ c flaked coconut

Combine first 6 ingredients; place in greased 1½ qt. baking dish. Combine brown sugar and flour; cut in butter until crumbly. Stir in nuts and coconut. Sprinkle over carrot mixture. Bake, uncovered, at 350° for 30 min. or until heated through.

Yield: 6-8 servings

Cheddar Baked Potato Slices

1 can (10¾ oz) cream of mushroom soup
½ t paprika
½ t pepper
4 med. baking potatoes cut into
        ¼ in slices (about 4 c)
1 c shredded cheddar cheese

In small bowl, combine soup, paprika and pepper. In a greased 2 qt oblong baking dish, arrange potatoes in overlapping rows. Sprinkle with cheese, spoon soup mixture over cheese. Cover with foil; bake at 400° for 45 min. Uncover; bake 10 min. or until potatoes are fork tender.

Makes 6 servings

Cheddar Potato Strips

3 large potatoes, cut into ½ in strips
½ c milk
1 T margarine
salt and pepper to taste
½ c shredded cheddar cheese
1 T minced fresh parsley

In a greased 9 x 13 in. baking dish, arrange potatoes in a single layer. Pour milk over potatoes. Dot with butter; sprinkle with salt and pepper. Cover and bake at 425° for 30 min. or until potatoes are tender. Sprinkle with cheese and parsley. Bake, uncovered, 5 min. longer or until cheese is melted.

Yield: 4 servings

Cheese Potato Casserole

2 lb frozen hash browns, thawed
½ c melted margarine
1 t salt
1 t pepper
1 c chopped onion
1 can cream of chicken soup
1 pt sour cream
2 c grated cheddar cheese

Combine all ingredients
Place in 9 x 13 in baking
dish. Bake 350° for
45 min. to 1 hour.

Cheesy Potato Casserole

1 (16 oz) processed Am. cheese, cubed
1 (32 oz) frozen hash browns, thawed
2 c mayonnaise
1 chopped onion
1 (3 oz) jar bacon bits

Preheat oven to 350°
In microwave, melt
cheese. Stir in potatoes,
mayonnaise and onion.
Spread in lightly greased
9 x 13 baking dish and
top with bacon bits.
Bake 1 hour or until
hot and bubbly.

Makes 12 servings

Cheesy Vegetable Casserole

1 (32 oz) bag frozen mixed vegetables
1 c chopped celery
⅓ c chopped onion
1 c mayonnaise
1 c shredded sharp cheddar cheese
½ t salt
Dash pepper
2 c cheese crackers, crushed
¼ c melted butter

Cook vegetables until barely tender; drain and combine with celery, onion, mayonnaise, ½ c of the cheese, salt and pepper. Place in a buttered casserole.

Top with crushed crackers; dribble with melted butter. Sprinkle with remaining ½ c cheese. Bake in 350° oven for about 30 min. or until hot and bubbly.

Makes 10-12 servings

Good!

Chili Beans

1 lb. ground beef
1 onion (chopped)
1 15 oz can tomatoes
1 can kidney beans
¼ T red pepper
2 T chili powder

Heat ground beef until gray and separated. Add onion, tomatoes and beans. Bring to a boil. Add red pepper, chili powder and salt to taste. Simmer one hour.

Serves 4

Cinnamon Apples

2 c water
¾ c red-hot candies
⅓ c sugar
6 med. tart apples, peeled
   and quartered

In a large saucepan, over medium heat, bring water candies and sugar to a boil, stirring constantly until candies and sugar are dissolved. Reduce heat; carefully add apples. Cook, uncovered, until apples are tender. Cool slightly. With a slotted spoon, transfer apples to a serving dish. Pour sugar syrup over apples. Cover and refrigerate for at least 3 hours.

Serves 6-8

Cole Slaw

3 c shredded cabbage
⅓ c mayonnaise
1 T vinegar
2 t sugar
½ t salt
½ t celery seed

Combine all ingredient Stir until sugar is dissolved.

Colorful Veggie Bake

2 pke (16oz) frozen California
    blend vegetables
8 oz Velvetta, cubed
6 T butter, divided
½ c crushed butter-flavored
    crackers (about 13)

Prepare vegetables according to
package directions. Place half in
an ungreased 7 X 11 baking dish.
In sauce pan, combine cheese and
4 T butter; cook and stir over
low heat until melted. Pour
half over vegetables. Repeat
layers.
Melt the remaining butter;
toss with crackers. Sprinkle
over top. Bake, uncovered, at
325° for 20-25 min. or until
golden brown.

Makes 8-10 servings

Walter B. Murphy

Company Potato Casserole

5 c cooked cubed peeled potatoes
1½ c (12z) sour cream
1¼ c shredded Swiss cheese, divided
½ c shredded carrot
¼ c chopped onion
2 T minced fresh parsley
1 t salt
½ t dill weed
¼ t pepper
¼ t paprika

Combine potatoes, sour cream,
1 c cheese, carrot, onion, parsley, salt,
dill and pepper. Transfer to a
greased 8 in. square baking
dish. Sprinkle with the paprika
and remaining cheese. Bake,
uncovered, at 350° for
25-35 min. or until bubbly.

Yield: 8 servings

Copper Carrots

2 lb. carrots
1 small green pepper
1 med. onion
1 can (10½ oz) tomato soup
1 t Worcestershire sauce
½ c salad oil
1 c sugar
¾ c vinegar
1 t prepared mustard
salt and pepper

Slice carrots and boil in salted water until tender. Drain and cool. Alternately layer carrots, green pepper and thin onion slices. Make a marinade of the remaining ingredients beating until completely blended. Pour over vegetables; cover and refrigerate.

This is best when allowed to chill for a few days. It will keep in the refrigerator for quite a while. Serve as a vegetable dish, a relish or as a dressing for a green salad.

Corn Casserole

1 can (16 oz) cream style corn
1 can (16 oz) corn kernels
1 (8½ oz) box corn muffin mix
1 c sour cream
1 egg

Preheat oven to 350°. Coat a 13 x 9 in baking dish with cooking spray.
In a large bowl, mix all ingredients until well-blended. Spoon into prepared baking dish. Bake for 30 min.

Dr. C.H. Richard's Baked Corn

1 can creamed corn
1 egg
1 heaping T flour
1 T butter or margarine
2 T sugar
⅓ c milk
1 c grated Cheddar cheese
12 saltine crackers, crushed and fried in butter

Mix first 6 ingredients together and pour into a baking dish. Top with crackers and cheese. Bake in a moderate oven about 30 min. or until set.

Duff's Sweet Potato Salad

4 c sweet potatoes, diced
½ c sugar
1 c heavy cream, whipped
1½ c miniature marshmallows
¼ t cinnamon

Drain potatoes in colander. Combine sugar, whipped cream, marshmallows and cinnamon in mixing bowl. Add drained potatoes. Mix very carefully when folding in potatoes so as not to crush them.

Place in large plastic container. Cover and store in refrigerator for later use.

Fried Green Tomatoes

1 egg
2 T milk
1 c flour
½ t salt
¼ t pepper
4 med. green tomatoes cut into ¼ in. slices
¼ c vegetable oil
1 T butter

In a shallow bowl, beat egg and milk. In another shallow bowl, mix the flour, salt and pepper. Pat tomatoes dry. Dip in egg mixture, then coat with the flour mix.

In a large skillet, heat oil and butter over med. high heat until butter is melted. Fry tomato slices, 4 at a time, 2-3 min. on each side or until golden brown. Drain on paper towels. Serve immediately.

Serves 6

Fried Onion Rings

1 qt oil
1 c flour
1 c beer
pinch salt
pinch pepper
4 large onion, peeled and
    sliced into rings)

In large deep skillet, heat oil to 375°. Combine flour, beer, salt and pepper in bowl. Mix until smooth. Dredge onion slices in batter until evenly coated. Deep-fry until golden brown. Drain on paper towels.

Makes 13 servings

Fried Squash

corn meal — 1 cup
flour — 2 T +
Sugar — 2 t
Salt — 1 t
Pepper — dash
corn starch — 1 T

Mix all together. Coat sliced squash and fry until golden in Canola oil.

Galax Delux Hashed Brown Potatoes

1 32 oz frozen hash browns
1 can cream of potato soup
1 can cream of celery soup
chopped onion and green pepper to taste
1 carton sour cream
salt and pepper
Parsley flakes
Paprika

Mix all ingredients except parsley and paprika together. Mix well. Place in lightly greased 9 X 13 in. dish. Sprinkle parsley and paprika on top.
Bake 300° oven 1½ - 2 hours.

Makes 12 servings

Ginnie Burton's Sweet Potato Balls

Cook potatoes fork tender. Drain. Stir up real good like mashed potatoes. While hot, add sugar (white or brown) butter, cinnamon and nutmeg. (Make it sweeter to taste than you want it in the end.)

Put the pan with the potatoes in the refrigerator and let them get good and cold.

Crush corn flakes to fine crumbs.

Take ½ marshmallow and mold potatoes around it to make a ball that will fit in your hand.

Roll in cornflake crumbs.

Fry in oil until brown.

Glazed Carrot Coins

2 T butter
2 T brown sugar
2 T orange juice
¼ t salt
¼ t ginger
⅛ t cinnamon
6 med. carrots cut in ½ in slices

In a small saucepan, melt butter over medium heat. Stir in brown sugar, orange juice, salt and ginger and cinnamon. Add the carrots; cover and cook for 20-25 min. or until tender, stirring occasionally.

Yield: 4 servings

Golden Corn Quiche

1 unbaked pastry shell (9 in.)
1⅓ c half and half cream
3 eggs
1 T butter, melted
½ small onion, diced
1 T flour
1 T sugar
1 t salt
2 c frozen corn, thawed

Line unpricked pastry shell with double thickness of heavy duty foil. Bake 375° for 5 min. Remove foil and bake 5 min. longer.

In blender, combine filling ingredients except corn. Cover and process until blended. Stir in corn and pour into crust. Bake 35 - 40 min. or until a knife inserted near center comes out clean. Let stand 10 min. before cutting.

Yield: 8 servings

Green Bean Casserole

2 cans (16 oz) cut green beans, drained
¾ c milk
1 can (10¾ oz) cream of mushroom soup
⅛ t black pepper
1 can (2.8 oz) French fried onions

Combine beans, milk, soup, pepper and ½ can onions; pour into 1½ qt. casserole dish. Bake, uncovered, at 350° for 30 min. Top with remaining onions and bake 5 min. longer.

Makes 6 servings

Ham and Broccoli Strata

12 slices white bread
8 slices sharp Am. cheese
3 c (or more) cooked ham, diced
8 eggs, beaten
4½ c milk
2 T minced onion
½ t salt
½ t dry mustard
1 c sharp Cheddar cheese

Cut circles of bread with biscuit cutter. Arrange in bottom of 13 X 9 in casserole. Place cheese slices over crusts covering all exposed parts. Spoon broccoli over cheese - Add ham. Arrange circles of bread on top making sure all ingredients are well covered with some overlapping necessary.

Combine eggs, milk, onion, salt, and mustard well. Pour over circles of bread making sure all are wet. Cover and refrigerate at least 6 hours.

Bake 325° for 55 min. or until well-browned all over. Five minutes before taking out of oven, sprinkle with sharp Cheddar cheese. Let stand 15 min before cutting.

Helen Dula's Cranberry Apples

3 c unpeeled tart apples, cubed.
2 c raw cranberries
Mix with ¾ c sugar

Top with
1 stick melted butter
1 c uncooked oatmeal
⅓ c flour
½ c brown sugar
½ c chopped nuts

Bake 1 hour in 350° oven

May be frozen and
baked later if desired.

Helen Dula's Squash

4 med. squash, sliced
2 chopped onions
salt
Cook until tender.
Add:
chunk of butter
about ¼ lb grated cheese
Bread crumbs about equal
to two hot dog rolls to
which enough milk is
added to make them
soft.

Mix all together and put
in greased baking dish.
Bake 350° for 30-40 min.

Can sprinkle a little cheese
or cracker crumbs on top
if desired.

Julie's Sweet Potato Casserole

4 c cooked mashed sweet potatoes
1½ c sugar
3 eggs - well beaten
2 t vanilla
1 t orange rind
⅓ c milk
½ c butter

Topping
1 c brown sugar
⅓ c butter
⅓ c flour
1 c chopped pecans

Combine sweet potatoes, sugar eggs, vanilla, orange rind, milk and ½ c butter. Beat until smooth. Spoon into greased 2 q casserole. Combine topping ingredients and sprinkle over the top. Bake at 350 for 30 min.

Loaded Potato Fans

4 large baking potatoes
2 T butter, melted
3 T grated Parmesan cheese
½ t dried rosemary, crushed
¼ t salt
⅛ t pepper
½ c shredded cheddar cheese
¼ c real bacon bits
1 green onion, chopped

Scrub potatoes. Slice thinly but not all the way through, leaving slices attached at the bottom. Place on microwave-safe plate; drizzle with butter. Combine Parmesan cheese, rosemary, salt and pepper; sprinkle over potatoes and between slices.

Microwave, uncovered, on high for 12-18 min. or until potatoes are tender. Top with cheddar cheese, bacon and onion. Microwave for 1-2 min. longer or until cheese is melted.

Makes 4 servings

Marjorie Petrou's Squash Casserole

2 lbs squash, sliced
1 med. onion, diced
1 med carrot, diced
2 T chopped pimento
½ c sour cream
1 can cream of chicken soup
1 pkg. Pepperidge Farm Herb Stuffing mix
1 stick margarine, melted

Cook squash, onions and carrots in small amount of water until tender. Drain well. Mash. Add sour cream, chicken soup, pimento and salt and pepper to taste, and half of the stuffing mix. Add ½ stick margarine to this mix and blend well. Put into a greased baking dish. Pour melted margarine over the other half of the stuffing and mix well. Put this on top of squash.

Bake 25 min covered in 375° oven. Serve hot.

Mildred Park's Corn Pudding

1 can cream style corn
3/4 c milk
2 eggs
1/4 c sugar
salt and pepper to taste
3 T flour
2 T softened butter

Combine all ingredients in a medium size mixing bowl. Beat well. Pour into a greased 1½ qt. oblong baking dish. Bake 45 min. at 350°.

Mildred Park's Stuffed Apples

Peel and core apples. Cook whole apples in a mix of
about ½ c sugar
"   2 c water
"   1 c cinnamon candy red hots
until apples are tender. Don't let them get too tender or they will fall apart.

Stuff with cream cheese moistened with milk and pineapple juice. Add some nuts, a little of the crushed pineapple and a few chopped maraschino cherries.

Moravian Ice Box Slaw

3 lbs. cabbage
2 green peppers
2 med. onions
1 4 oz jar chopped pimentos
1 T salt
2 T mustard seed

Grate or chop vegetables. Add salt and mustard seed.

In a sauce pan combine
2 c vinegar
2 c water
2 c sugar
Heat, stirring until mixture comes to a boil and sugar is dissolved.

Cool and pour over cabbage mixture. Let stand in refrigerator 24 hours.

Slaw keeps a long time under refrigeration.

Good!

Opal's Broccoli-Cheese Casserole

2 (10oz) frozen broccoli spears
1 (10oz) sharp cheddar cheese
½ stick margarine
1 c Ritz crackers, rolled fine

Melt cheese and margarine in top of double boiler. Cook broccoli until tender. Arrange in 2 qt casserole dish starting with broccoli, then melted cheese and margarine, then Ritz crackers. Finish with crackers on top. Bake at 325° for 30 min.

Orange Candied Carrots

1 lb bag carrots, sliced
¼ c butter
½ c jellied cranberry sauce
¼ c orange juice
3 T brown sugar
½ t salt

Put all in a large pot. Add water to cover carrots. Cook until tender.

Parmesan Baked Potatoes

6 T margarine, melted
3 T grated Parmesan cheese
8 med. unpeeled red potatoes
(about 2¾ lb) halved lengthwise

Pour butter into a 13x9 baking pan. Sprinkle cheese over butter. Place potato with cut side down over cheese. Bake, uncovered, at 400° for 40-45 min. or until tender.

Yield: 6 servings.

Party Carrots

2 lb. carrots, sliced
2 t chicken bouillon granules
6 oz Velvetta cheese, cubed
2 T butter
1 (8 oz) cream cheese, cubed
4 green onions, sliced
¼ t salt
¼ t pepper

In 1 in water bring carrots and bouillon to boil. Reduce heat. Cover and simmer 7-9 min. or until crisp tender.

In another pan, combine cheese and butter. Cook and stir over low heat until melted. Add cream cheese, onions, salt and pepper. Cook and stir until cream cheese is melted.

Drain the carrots; stir into the cheese sauce. Transfer to a greased shallow 2 qt. baking dish. Cover and bake at 350° for 20-25 min. or until bubbly.

Yield: 8 servings

Picnic Bean Casserole

2 cans (15 g) pork and beans
1 can (16 g) kidney beans, drained and rinsed
1 can (15 g) lima or butter beans, drained and rinsed
1 medium onion, chopped
½ c packed brown sugar
½ c ketchup
4 bacon strips, cooked and crumbled

In a large bowl, combine the beans, onion, brown sugar and ketchup. Transfer to a greased 2½ qt. baking dish. Sprinkle with bacon. Cover and bake at 350° for 1 hour. Uncover and bake 30 min. longer.

Yield: 10 servings

Pineapple Au Gratin

2 (20 g) cans pineapple chunks
1 c sugar
6 T flour
2 c sharp cheddar cheese, grated
2 c cheese Nips crackers, crushed
1 stick butter, melted

Drain pineapple and save the juice. In a bowl, mix together sugar, flour, 8 T pineapple juice till well blended. Mix pineapple chunks and cheese. Pour into 1½ qt casserole (9 x 13) sprayed with Pam. Mix crushed cheese Nips with melted butter in a bowl. Place on top of casserole. Bake at 350° for 30 - 40 min or until hot and bubbly.

Good!

Potato Casserole

1 (32 oz) frozen hash browns, thawed
1 can cream of chicken soup
1 (8 oz) sour cream
2 T onion flakes
1 t salt
12 oz grated sharp cheese

Mix together and pour into a large flat casserole dish. Crush 2 c cornflakes and mix with ½ c melted margarine. Crumble over potato mixture. Bake 350° for 30 min. covered. Bake an additional 15 minutes uncovered.

10 – 12 servings

Potatoes O'Brien

5 c cubed cooked potatoes
   (about 6 medium sized)
3 T finely chopped onion
3 T chopped pimento
1 c condensed cheddar cheese soup
⅓ c milk
1 t salt
1 T fine dry bread crumbs

Heat oven to 350°. Combine potatoes, onion and pimento and place in lightly greased 1½ qt. casserole dish. Combine cheese soup, milk and salt. Pour over potatoes. Sprinkle top with bread crumbs. Bake uncovered 30 min. until heated through.

Serves 4 – 6

Ranch-Style Baked Beans

2 T margarine
1 lb ground chuck
1 onion soup mix
2 (16 oz) cans pork and beans
1 (16 oz) can kidney beans, drained
1 c ketchup
½ c cold water
2 T prepared mustard
2 T cider vinegar

Preheat oven to 400°. In large skillet, melt margarine and brown meat. Stir in remaining ingredients. Mix well.

Pour into a 2½ qt. casserole. Bake 30-45 min. until hot and bubbly.

Makes 8-10 servings

Good!

Scored Potatoes

4 large baking potatoes
2 T margarine, melted, divided
⅛ t paprika
1 T minced fresh parsley
Salt and pepper to taste

With a sharp knife, cut potatoes in half lengthwise. Slice each half widthwise six times but not all the way through; fan potatoes slightly. Place in a shallow baking dish.

Brush potatoes with 1 T margarine. Sprinkle with paprika, parsley, salt and pepper. Bake, uncovered, at 350° for 50 min. or until tender. Drizzle with the remaining margarine.

Yield: 4 servings

Shoepeg Corn Casserole

2 cans (11 oz) shoepeg corn, drained
1 can (10¾ oz) cream of celery soup, undiluted
1 (8 oz) sour cream
1 c shredded Cheddar cheese
½ c chopped onion
½ c chopped celery
¼ c chopped green pepper
¾ c crushed buttery crackers
2 T margarine, melted

In a large bowl, combine the first 7 ingredients. Transfer to a greased 2 qt. baking dish. Sprinkle with the cracker crumbs. Drizzle with margarine. Bake, uncovered, at 350° for 20-25 min. or until bubbly.

Yield: 6 servings

Southern Slaw

1 head cabbage, shredded
1 c chopped dill pickles
¾ c chopped onion
1 c mayonnaise
2 T mustard
2 t sugar
1 t celery seed
2 t vinegar
⅛ t pepper

Combine vegetables and mix well. Combine other ingredients and mix well. Pour over cabbage mixture and mix well. Chill, covered 4-6 hours.

Makes 14-16 servings

Spiced Apples

¼ c butter
4 large Granny Smith apples
    peeled, cored and sliced
¾ c sugar
¾ t cinnamon
¼ t nutmeg

Melt butter in large skillet over med.-high heat. Add apples and other ingredients. Saute 15 min. or until apples are tender.

Spiced Peaches

½ c sugar
½ c water
¼ c vinegar
8-10 whole cloves
1 stick cinnamon
6 fresh peaches, peeled and halved
½ c sour cream
2 T brown sugar

Bring first 5 ingredients to a boil. Reduce heat; simmer 10 min. Add peaches; simmer for about 10 min. or until heated through. Discard cinnamon stick; pour into a shallow baking dish. Cover and chill 8 hours or overnight. Drain. Spoon peaches into serving dishes; garnish with a dollop of sour cream and sprinkle with brown sugar.

Yield: 6 servings

Squash Casserole

2 c diced squash
½ c grated cheese
½ c cracker crumbs
½ stick butter
1 egg
1 c milk
salt and pepper

Cook squash until tender.
Drain and add cheese, cracker
crumbs, butter, eggs, milk
and salt and pepper. Pour
into dish and bake 350°
until brown and firm —
about 30 min.

Stuffed Baked Potatoes

3 large baking potatoes
1½ t vegetable oil
½ c sliced green onions
½ c margarine, divided
½ c light cream
½ c sour cream
1 t salt
½ t white pepper
1 c shredded cheddar cheese
Paprika

Rub potatoes with oil and pierce
with a fork. Bake 400° 1hr. or until
tender. Cool to touch. Cut in half lengthwise
and scoop out pulp leaving a thin shell.

Place pulp in large bowl. Saute onions
in ¼ c margarine until tender. Add to potato
pulp light cream, sour cream, salt and
pepper. Beat until smooth. Fold in cheese.
Stuff shells and place in 9 X 13 in pan.
Melt remaining butter and drizzle
over potatoes. Sprinkle with paprika.
Bake at 350° for 20-30 min or until
heated through.

Yield: 6 servings

Sweet Potato Balls

2½ c mashed canned or cooked
   sweet potatoes (18 oz can or 2 lbs fresh)
½ t salt
Dash pepper
2 T margarine, melted
½ c honey
1 T margarine
1 c chopped pecans

Combine potatoes, salt, pepper
and 2 T margarine; chill. Shape
into 8 balls. Heat honey and 1 T
margarine in small skillet
over high heat. When syrup
is hot, remove from heat; add
potato balls, one at a time.
Spoon glaze over, coating completely.
Roll in chopped nuts. Place
balls so they do not touch each
other in a greased shallow
baking dish. Bake at 350°
for 20-25 min.

Sweet Potato Casserole with Crunchy Topping

3 c mashed sweet potatoes
1 c sugar
½ t salt
⅓ stick margarine, melted
½ c evaporated milk
2 eggs, beaten
1 t butter flavoring
1 t vanilla
½ - 1 t cinnamon

Cream all ingredients and turn into greased baking dish.

Topping
1 c brown sugar
⅓ c flour
⅓ stick margarine
½ - 1 c chopped pecans

Blend together and sprinkle on top of casserole. Bake in a 325° oven for 20-25 min.

(can be made 3 days ahead.)

Sweet Potato Casserole

Mash 6-7 sweet potatoes, boiled in jackets
cooled and peeled OR 1 large can
of sweet potatoes

Add ¾ stick margarine
½ c sugar
¼ c brown sugar
¼ c canned milk
2 eggs
cinnamon, nutmeg and vanilla to taste
1-2 c coconut

Mix these ingredients well and
pour into a casserole dish.

Top With 1 c crushed corn flakes
¾ stick melted margarine
½ c brown sugar
¼ c pecans

Bake at 450° for 15 min.

Variation: For topping use
1 c brown sugar
⅓ c flour
1 c nuts
⅓ stick melted margarine

Sweet Potato Puffs

1 c plain mashed sweet potatoes
1 T brown sugar
¼ t salt
⅛ t cinnamon
6 large marshmallows
⅓-½ c graham cracker crumbs

Combine sweet potato, brown
sugar, salt and cinnamon;
shape a small amount
around each marshmallow.
Roll in crumbs. Place on a
greased baking sheet. Bake
at 350° for 6 min. or
until lightly puffed.

Yield: 2 servings

Three Bean Casserole

2 bacon strips, diced
1 large green pepper, chopped
1 med. onion, chopped
1 (31 oz) can pork and beans
1 (16 oz) can kidney beans, rinsed and drained
1 (15¼ oz) can lima beans, rinsed and drained
½ c ketchup
1 (4 oz) jar diced pimentos
¼ c packed brown sugar
1 T Worcestershire sauce
1 t ground mustard

Cook bacon until crisp. Reserve 1 T drippings and saute pepper and onions in it until tender. Combine beans and gently stir in pepper, onion and bacon. Stir in ketchup, pimentos, brown sugar, Worcestershire and mustard until combined. Transfer to a 2 qt. baking dish coated with Pam, cover and bake 350° for 50-60 min. or until bubbly.

Serves 9

To Freeze Corn
N.C. State Agriculture Lady

Cut corn off of the cob.
Put in a pot and barely
cover with water. Bring
to a full, rolling boil and
then turn off heat.
Set it off and let it
get cold.
Put in containers and
freeze. Can use plastic
containers or Ziploc bags.

Toddle House Hash Browns

Baking potatoes
Vegetable oil
Paprika
Salt and pepper

Bake potatoes. When done and
cool enough to handle, peel and
dice.
In a sautepan over medium
heat, put about 2 T vegetable
oil or enough to prevent
potatoes from sticking.
When oil is hot, measure
1 c diced potatoes, add them
to pan and sprinkle with
enough paprika to give them
a nice color.
Flip and fry potatoes
until golden brown. Serve
hot with salt and pepper
to taste,

Tomato Pie

1 unbaked deep dish pie shell
3 - 5 tomatoes
10 cooked and crumbled bacon strips
1 c shredded cheese
1 c mayonnaise
1 c sliced onion
Season with rosemary and garlic

Bake pastry shell and then cool. Place tomatoes in the crust along with sliced onion. Season accordingly. Sprinkle with bacon. Mix cheeses and mayonnaise together. Spoon over bacon, spreading and leaving about an inch around the edge without cheese spread.

Bake 350° for 30 - 40 min. or until golden brown.

This is really good with corn on the cob and salad.

Made in the USA
San Bernardino, CA
27 April 2017